I0568360

Mastering Your Anxious Brain

*Overcome Negative Thoughts and Lack of Focus,
and Rewire Your Brain with Positivity*

BY

Jasmine O' Brien

Koala Publishers

Disclaimer Notice

This book is written and published independently. Please keep in mind that the material in this publication is solely for educational and entertaining purposes. All efforts have provided authentic, up-to-date, trustworthy, and comprehensive information. There are no express or implied assurances. The purpose of this book's material is to assist readers in having a better understanding of the subject matter. The activities, information, and exercises are provided solely for self-help information. This book is not intended to replace expert psychologists, legal, financial, or other guidance. If you require counseling, please get in touch with a qualified professional.

By reading this text, the reader accepts that the author will not be held liable for any damages, indirectly or directly, experienced due to the use of the information included herein, particularly, but not limited to, omissions, errors, or inaccuracies. As a reader, you are accountable for your decisions, actions, and consequences.

About the Author

Jasmine O' Brien is a child psychiatrist with a deep understanding of child behavior and mental illnesses. She has spent more than 8 years in the field helping tons of children suffering from anxiety, depression, chronic stress, phobias, and much more. She also has years-long experience as the parent of a child with GAD (Generalized Anxiety Disorder.) She understands the helplessness of parenting a child with anxiety and hopes to help parents like these on a broader scale with her professional expertise.

"Anxiety Control for Kids" is one of her famous marvels on parenting kids with troubled psychology and behavior, among many other educational and interactive books.

Table of contents

Introduction

Even if you are facing anxiety issues in your life, you need not worry at all. We are making this statement with such huge confidence due to the latest developments in the medical industry, availability of modern relaxation techniques, tried & tested therapies and multiple daily life practices as recommended by the experts in the field.

What do you think is meant by the anxious brain? Do you have any idea regarding the issues related to negativity? Even if you don't have any idea about such concepts, we will discuss them all with you and the best possible solutions.

So, before we jump in to understand all the complex concepts related to anxiety and the working of the human brain, let us start with the very basics. According to the definition, anxiety is "a sensation of worry, apprehension, or unease over something like an unclear consequence." Our brains are basic, meant to protect us from injury and peril.

Anxiety can be beneficial in some instances by keeping us safe. For instance, don't put your hand in a fire since it will burn you or remain inside during a storm.

When anxiety becomes a problem, it hinders us from doing activities we normally enjoy and need to do, such as going to work or buying, or when we are afraid to visit new locations and meet different friends.

Mastering your mind, heart, and spirit may help you overcome the consequences of stress, anxiety, or even pride to achieve better health outcomes and ultimate success in every situation. All it needs is several simple tools.

Perhaps your bad thoughts have blossomed into something new as you try to understand the behavioral changes that are causing emotional repercussions and, as a result, physical harm to your health.

To become a master, you must abandon narrow-minded methods and become an accomplished student. It is feasible to clear your brain of anything that does not serve you and substitute it with abilities and realistic daily routines that exclusively serve your objectives.

The book "**Mastering your Anxious Brain**" is a comprehensive piece of writing that will highlight all the important aspects necessary to keep your mind positive throughout your life. After all, we are humans, and we can come across many testing situations in our lives. The question arises, how can we tackle such situations positively? It is because staying positive in difficult conditions will bring us all the good in the long run. On the other hand, if we take such situations to our heart and let anxiety and depression take over, we will soon experience negativity. The need is to look for the reasons that force us to have anxious thoughts. The next step should try to minimize all such factors from our lives.

The cells in our brains produce a positive mindset. We have to grasp how our brain works to comprehend how good and unfavorable feelings affect our mentality. The hippocampus in our brain regulates our feelings. The amygdala governs and reacts to pleasant and depressive moods, such as joy and worry or despair. Positive thoughts alter brain wiring, influencing specific genes and perhaps changing brain cells. Genetic change is a trigger for human well-being and that of coming generations. Positivity is also linked to increases in immune-system-boosting cells. Positive energy, in essence, is a soldier who defends your body and mind from negative influences. Good feelings act as a buffer against negative feelings like sadness and post-traumatic stress disorder.

The chemistry of our brain influences how we think. When we think positive or feel cheerful, cortisol levels drop, and the brain produces dopamine in reaction. Normal serotonin levels make you feel joyful, relaxed, less stressed, more focused, and mentally stable.

We can't be happy all of the time. We all experience emotions like tension, depression, and anxiety from time to time. These feelings influence how we react to our surroundings and our dear ones. Our surroundings have a significant impact on how we see our society and the success of our lives. When exposed to bad events such as unemployment, lack of love, violence, or mistreatment, our brain chemistry changes.

On their road to happiness, everyone takes a very different path. Healing requires us to discover how we feel at ease. We sometimes do not know where to start while looking for healthy behaviors. We may be unaware of the source of our unpleasant thoughts or sentiments in some circumstances. Joining groups dedicated to reducing harmful behavior patterns is a good start when looking for answers. Members of the group will share their stories and offer assistance. Those who work in groups understand how tough selecting and adopting a healthy lifestyle is. Accept the advice of a mentor, somebody you feel comfortable speaking with.

Positive thinking has several advantages. When we participate in positive thinking, we experience joy in our lives or others. Our nervous system and actions are affected by emotional states. Positive thinking will help you be more creative, keep focused, resolve issues faster, and be more productive. On the other hand, negative thoughts might cause slower reaction times, memory loss, and a loss of impulse control. Environmental elements we encounter as children or adults can contribute to a negative outlook. Our mindset is also influenced by genetics.

Cutting things short, it is important to help your mind think only in a positive direction as it will ultimately affect your whole life. Several daily life activities can impart much-needed positivity and relaxation to your mind and body. Furthermore, if the level of anxiety is bigger than expectations, you can also take the help of the experts. Multiple therapies can help you tackle issues like anxiety, depression, or a constant state of sadness.

If you have any such issues or detect something like this in your loved ones, now is the time to read the book to completely understand the issue. As you will go along different chapters, you will also be able to learn multiple positivity-enhancing tips and techniques. Follow the insights discussed in the book and act upon the instructions as much as possible.

Chapter 1: Understanding Anxiety & Depression

We live in a fast-paced world where everyone struggles to get ahead of others in today's competitive environment. When you remain in a constant state of competition and comparison, negative things are bound to happen. It is a common perception that anxiety and depression are the products of the 21st century, and the statement is not true to a certain extent. Such issues have been there in the past, too, and there are numerous other reasons behind the growth of such mental disorders. Before we discuss these complex concepts, let us start with the basics of anxiety and depression.

1.1 What is Anxiety?

Anxiety is a natural human sentiment that marks every one of us at some point in our lives. Anxiety supports us in identifying and replying to danger. It can stimulate us to face our worries and take on thought-provoking tasks. Anxiety in a calculated quantity can help us achieve better and inspire achievement and creativity. There is, nevertheless, another side to nervousness. Regular anxiety produces important mental pain and, in the worst-case situation, can lead to ailment and the growth of anxiety syndromes such as terror attacks, fears, and compulsive behaviors.

Nervousness at this level can have an upsetting effect on our lives and our physical and psychological health. Some experts have named our time "The Era of Anxiety." A poll specially made by the Mental Health Foundation settles this impression of universal concern. Disturbingly, nearly one-fifth of respondents have said they are nervous almost all of the time. It has also been noticed that people are more worried today than a few years ago.

Anxiety is one of the most predominant mental health issues globally, and it is continuously on the rise. Despite this, it is under-reported, misdiagnosed, and untreated. A capable aptitude to compete with nervousness is essential for flexibility in the face of life's encounters. Nevertheless, if we have too much of it, we risk being shocked and powerless to find equilibrium in our lives and relax as much as possible. Our aptitude to determine inner peace has never been more life-threatening to our general health.

It is also about overpowering the humiliation that still stops us from looking for treatment and support when our anxiety stages become a considerate concern. We need to better comprehend and be involved with anxiety as individuals, recognizing when it is carefully alerting us to pay consideration and having coping approaches in place when negative inspiration becomes too strong.

It is a natural response to strain that can be helpful in certain conditions. It can caution us of imminent threats and support us in preparation and paying attention. Anxiety conditions are marked by excessive fear or nervousness, contrasting with normal sentiments of uneasiness or anxiety. These disorders are the most prevalent mental ailments, affecting about one-third of all grownups at some point in their lives. However, such disorders are treatable, and various operative treatments are available. The majority of the sufferers who obtain treatment successfully get normal, productive lives.

Anxiety is characterized by muscle stiffness and evasive behavior in anticipation of a future worry. Terror is an expressive response to an imminent threat that is usually more associated with a fight or flight reply. People with nervousness disorders may try to evade circumstances that gun trigger or aggravate their symptoms. Office performance, homework, and personal associations may all be impacted.

Anxiety is a prevalent incidence in people's lives. People with anxiety syndromes usually experience harsh, excessive, and obstinate concern and terror in usual settings. Anxiety disorders are often characterized by recurrent episodes of acute nervousness, horror, or fear.

Such conditions can disturb daily life mechanisms, be problematic to control, be out of proportion to the definite risk, and last long. To evade unpleasant feelings, you may avoid certain places or conditions. Signs may appear in childhood or adolescence and persist throughout adulthood.

It is normal to experience some unrest. If you come face to face with a problem at work, going to a conference, taking an examination, or making a major choice, you may feel concerned or stressed.

If you have an anxiety condition, you may come across terror all of the time. It is penetrating and can be incapacitating at times. This nervousness may force you to say no to happenings that you like. If anxiety is not handled in the real sense of the word, it will only get worse.

Anxiety disorders are the most recurrent type of expressive disorder, upsetting people of all ages. Women are more expected than men to be identified with anxiety disorders, as per the American Psychiatric Association.

Types of Anxiety Disorders

Have you ever speculated why you trembled before an exam or why your palms got sweat during a job meeting? Nervousness is the body's usual way of communicating for a big event. You may have also seen that you started to calm yourself down; your heart stopped beating, and you initiated to respire more effortlessly. Because anxiety makes us concentrate more, it sometimes helps us accomplish better.

On the other hand, some people agonize from apprehension or panic affairs for no deceptive reason. If you have trouble governing your doubts and these repeated emotions of nervousness interfere with your aptitude to carry out daily errands, you may have an anxiety condition.

Because everyone gets a feeling of anxiety, it is problematic to determine when it is recognized as an anxiety condition. You should get help from a mental health expert if your doubts and anxiety become debilitating. Anxiety has various effects on people, resulting in a wide range of diseases. Some of the types of anxiety disorders are discussed as under.

Generalized Anxiety Disorder (GAD)

GAD patients have a lot of nervousness and concern about many dissimilar things. They fight with unease, apprehension, impatience, and a constant sense of being on edge. There is no exact trigger for such people who are not worried about anything.

Obsessive-Compulsive Disorder (OCD)

It is a psychological sickness that affects people and sufferers overwhelmed by anxiety-inducing feelings and apprehensions. They get rid of their fear by doing similar things repeatedly. An individual who is frightened of microorganisms and contamination, for example, will wash their hands and utensils daily and that too, multiple times a day.

Social Anxiety Disorder

It is a condition in which a person is frightened of social environments. People affected by social anxiety conditions are scared of being mediated in community and demonstration circumstances. They are horrified by shame or awkwardness as a result of whatsoever they do or say. These people can't get control and a firm grip on simple errands like making a small presentation or eating in public.

Exclusive Phobias

Phobias are speculative anxieties, and those who suffer from them will take substantial measures to evade the object or situation that causes them apprehension. Flying in planes, being in packed places, and even inoffensive things like spiders and taller buildings are likely the sources of fear and terror.

Post-Traumatic Stress Disorder (PTSD)

It is a psychological condition that can happen after some accident, calamity or a military battle. Being a part of or observing a shocking event, such as an accident or an attack, can result in post-traumatic stress disorder. Because of the incident's continual memories, the person can find it hard to sleep well or relax properly.

Anxiety Attacks

People with panic conditions have uncontrollable panic attacks that include faintness, shortness of breath, and heavy perspiration, among other physical indications. They also label psychological symptoms such as a sense of approaching doom and negative feelings. These spells seem to occur for no outward reason, and the victim afterward lives in repeated terror of another attack.

If you have a family member or friend who is a victim of anxiety conditions, your assistance can help them feel well. The first step, like with any illness, is to learn about the victim's problem so that you can sympathize with them. Working with people who have anxiety conditions involves a lot of tolerance, but they also need to be hard-pressed and stimulated to challenge their worries or fears from time to time to get them under control.

You can develop a variety of approaches to help you cope with anxiety. People generally employ strategies such as optimistic thinking, stress organization, accepting a healthy lifestyle, and comforting. Trying to get a hold of nervousness on your own can be tough, particularly if you are in a lot of discomfort. In such circumstances, seeking specialized help is typically a smart idea.

1.2 What is Depression? Are Anxiety & Depression Similar Terms?

Depression, commonly known as a main depressive syndrome, is an attitude illness that causes you to feel hopeless or impassive in life consistently. Most people come across sadness or sorrow from time to time. It is a natural response to anguish or life's complications. Nevertheless, when severe sorrow lasts for days to weeks and stops you from perfectly living your life, it may be much more than depression. Clinical depression is a medical condition that can be taken care of by taking due help from specialists.

It is a mental ailment categorized by a determined sense of sadness and loss of attention. It is not similar to the mood swings that everyone happens to go through regularly. Grief or the loss of a job are instances of major life happenings that can contribute to unhappiness. On the other hand, doctors only deliberate heartbreak to be a reason for unhappiness if it continues.

It is a longstanding subject, not a glitch on the radar. It comprises events with indications that last at least two weeks. It ultimately affects how you feel, contemplate, and act and can lead to several psychological and physical complications.

It is also known as a major depressive condition or clinical depression. You may find it hard to carry out daily tasks, and you may feel as if life isn't worth living.

Despair or depression is more than just a case of sadness, and it isn't approximately you can get rid of that easily. It may require long-term rehabilitation. Medication, psychotherapy, or both aid most people in misery. An individual's anguish might be aggravated by the demise of a loved one, the loss of an occupation, or the end of a relationship.

Nevertheless, anxiety is not entirely the same as depression. Grief is a usual and distinct process that parts some of the same features as depression. Anguish and depression can cause life-threatening dejection and extraction from daily life mechanisms. They are also dissimilar in several ways: In grief, painful sentiments come in waves, regularly merged with happy memories of the dead.

Self-confidence is regularly well-maintained during anxiety. Feelings of insignificance and self-blaming are characteristic of thoughtful unhappiness. In serious unhappiness, feelings turn to take one's life because one feels valueless or undeserving of living or because one is powerless to manage the suffering of despair.

If we talk about it from a broader perspective, anxiety and depression are two feelings that can coexist. It is important to differentiate between grieving and depression so that people can get the assistance, provision, and handling they require. Though unhappiness and grieving share some features, depression is dissimilar from grief faced after the death of a loved one or sadness experienced succeeding a sore life happening. Grief does not regularly involve self-blaming or a loss of self-esteem, whereas depression does.

Optimistic feelings and good memories of the dead are common signs to spirits of emotional sorrow and grief. The feelings of sadness are incessant in the chief depressive condition. Depression establishes itself in a diversity of ways for numerous people. It may cause disturbances in your unvarying routine, resulting in lost time and decreased production. It can also influence associations and some long-lasting illnesses.

Depression comprises various types, and all of them can be cured in one way or another. In order to look for the problems, we need to understand the issues first. The following passage will tell you about some common depression-related disorders.

Major Depressive Disorder (MDD)

It is one of the most common depressive disorders found in people from all over the world. However, the good thing is that it can be cured with the help of specialists and other healthy habits and lifestyles. It is characterized by imperative or overwhelming indications that endure more than two weeks. These indications make it difficult to go about your daily routine.

Bipolar Depression

If we talk about another noteworthy type from the list of common depression conditions, then the name Bipolar Depression will be placed at the top of the list. People with such an issue come face to face with stages of low mood followed by intermissions of great energy. They may come across depression indications such as sadness, desperation, or a lack of energy.

Perinatal and Postpartum Depression

"Perinatal" directly denotes the time that starts from the birth of a child. Postpartum unhappiness is a type that many people use to label this sort of depression. Perinatal despair can attack during pregnancy and last for up to a year subsequent to the birth of a child. The child's dejections, which persuade sensible melancholy, anxiety, or stiffness, are not the only signs.

Premenstrual Dysphoric Disorder

As the name suggests, it is related to a medical condition of the women and is a much more severe form of premenstrual illness. It generally has effects on women for days or weeks following a menstrual cycle.

The list of depression disorders goes on and on, and people can come across several different conditions in this regard. However, every type of depressive condition is to be treated with the help of experts having different types of abilities. In short, depression is curable, and it should be targeted at the earliest to keep the damage done to the minimum.

1.3 Causes of Anxiety

Anxiety is not only prevalent but also vital for existence when

an individual is challenged with possibly harmful or terrifying causes. Since the beginning of evolution, the method of predators and approaching danger has set off fears in the body, permitting evasive acts. These alerts display a quicker heartbeat, sweat, and enhanced sympathy for the environment.

The haste of adrenalin, a hormone and biochemical messenger in the brain, is released in reply to a threat, activating these nervous behaviors in a procedure known as the "fight-or-flight" reply. This makes people face or flee any possible hazards to their safety.

Running away from bigger creatures and looming danger is a less persuasive worry for many people than for early humans. Anxiety today affects work, cash, household life, well-being, and other significant matters that request a person's consideration but do not require a quick and instant response.

The anxiety you get before a big occasion or in a demanding scenario is a natural resonance of your body's unique response. It might nonetheless be essential for existence - for example, fear of getting into a car accident when crossing the street causes a person to have a look both ways to evade danger. Apprehension can be brought by a mental disease, a physical illness, pharmacological side impacts, demanding life events, or a grouping of these factors. The doctor's first responsibility is to identify whether your nervousness indicates another medical problem.

Normal anxiety is not identical to intense anxiety conditions. They are the most recurrent type of mental disorder in the United States and even worldwide, bothering roughly one out of every five persons. They can comprise intense anxiety or fear sessions above what you imagine with normal conditions.

Anxiety and depression can disturb daily tasks, be tough to regulate, and last for a long time. To evade unfriendly feelings, you may evade certain places or conditions. Symptoms may come forward in childhood and persist throughout adulthood.

It is important to watch the potential causes behind anxiety and depression to understand the real issue at hand. It will help us get a hold of the causes, and we will be able to keep the damage to the minimum.

Medical Reasons

Along with several other reasons, the name of medical causes will always remain at the top of the list as it has a major effect on all of us. Multiple symptoms of depression are coming forward due to serious health issues, and one needs to get a medical check-up done regularly to keep a check on any such issues.

Diabetes and heart diseases are the reasons behind several problems. When a person has diabetes, he will not be able to eat sweet-natured food items freely as it would seriously impact the patient's life. It can directly cause depression as they think that there is no excitement left in their life. The same goes true for other heart diseases and respiratory disorders whose intensity increases when a person is in a state of depression and vice versa.

Suppose a person is highly dependent on drug usage and is told to minimize such practices by the doctor. Despite the negative impacts that can be brought to him from drug misuse, the person will not be able to perform his daily life activities perfectly due to excessive dependence on the overdosed drugs.

Risky Matters

Apart from the medical-related issues, we can see several daily reasons as potential causes of anxiety and depression in human beings. It can be caused due to the trauma faced by the children during their early childhood. Getting sexual exploitation or facing abandonment from a family member can be the most relevant reasons in such a scenario. Similarly, the personality of a person also matters a lot. If the person is not confident enough, they will not be able to face the incoming challenges with an open heart. Such a situation will bring in unwanted depression to a greater extent.

Similarly, if any of your family members or friends are going through such disorders, it is highly likely that you will also get affected. Lastly, the issues of depression don't come up suddenly as there is a series of events that ultimately become a reason for such unwanted conditions.

1.4 Impacts of Anxiety & Depression

Almost all of us suffer from nervousness or sadness at some point. It is a characteristic "fight or flight" reply that helps you grip a hazardous or demanding situation with extra caution or attention in the right circumstances. When faced with stimulating, life-changing circumstances, it is normal to feel isolated, unfortunate, or impassive.

It is no longer ordinary when nervousness affects daily living and feelings of irresistible downheartedness or emptiness stay there for a longer period as these are severe mental issues. If we talk specifically about the United States alone, such disorders are the most common mental issue as almost 20% of the adult population is already affected.

Untreated nervousness or depressive conditions can affect more than just your everyday life; they can also influence your physical well-being, either by worsening existing health issues or causing noteworthy problems to develop.

Continuous anxiety is an expressive reaction, but opinions of concern or terror can also activate a physical response. When you are concerned, your neurotransmitters send these indications to your understanding of the nervous system, which causes your muscles to contract and your heart rate and breathing to rise. Blood flow from your abdominal body parts to your brain is also readdressed.

When anxiety develops into the rule rather than the exemption, its physical properties might become more noticeable, resulting in indications such as dizziness, abdominal pain, and a fast-resting heart rate.

Digestive Disorder

Continual anxiety can make you sick to your digestive system, resulting in stomach cramps or continuing digestive complications such as gas pains, diarrhea, or constipation. All of this is because nervousness directly affects your nervous system, and your nervous system directly influences your intestines.

Irritable bowel syndrome (IBS) is also associated with chronic anxiety. The nerves that hold the control of digestion are oversensitive to stimulus in both of these diseases. It is predicted that nearly half of persons with IBS also come face to face with anxiety.

Coronary Artery Disease

It is common among medical experts that anxiety directly impacts heart health. According to studies, having an untreated anxiety problem upsurges your risk of evolving heart disease. Persistent anxiety can raise your risk of heart attack or stroke if you previously had heart disease.

Adults with heart issues and an anxiety disorder are two times more likely to suffer a heart attack than individuals with heart disease but no anxiety disorder.

Central Nervous System

If disorders like anxiety and depression stay with you for a longer time, the chances are higher that these will ultimately impact your brain and central nervous system. The whole of your thinking process will be affected, and you will not be able to make decisions with an open mind. There are likelihoods that you will come across dizziness and headaches on a common basis and be in a state of apprehension.

When you are concerned or disturbed, your brain sends messages and chemicals to your nervous system to help you reply to a danger. While strain hormones can be helpful for the rare high-stress happening, long-term experience with them can be critical to your physical health.

Immune System

If you are anxious and stressed consistently or for a lengthy period, your body will never accept the signal to go back to normal functioning. This can cause your body's immunity to depreciate, making you more vulnerable to viral contaminations and diseases. Moreover, your usual vaccinations may not perform as well if you have anxiety.

Chapter 2: Anxiety & Brain

When discussing the anxiety and depression of the humans around us, including ourselves, the discussion should revolve around the human brain. It is because certain changes in the thinking process play an important role in bringing unwanted conditions like anxiety and sadness. The human brain directly relates to such issues, and it has been proved with the help of the latest research works from experts in the medical fields that study the working of the central nervous system. If you are looking for the best possible solution to such issues, you need to understand the problem by going through the technical reasons. This chapter is all about the relationship of the brain with anxiety disorders.

2.1 How Does Anxiety Affect Your Brain?

All of us might have been victims of depression, fear, and nervousness. Terror is an expressive response to a dangerous inducement. On the other hand, anxiety is a less strong enduring reaction to recognized anxiety-inducing stimuli. For example, you might be concerned about coming across a snake on a forest journey and you may be frightened if one slid right in front of you.

People can become anxious for no seeming reason in some conditions. Fear and nervousness are usually handled by the brain so that they do not inhibit our daily lives. When we are challenged with a hazard, diverse parts of our brain support us in making sense of it by expanding or reducing our nervousness and fear.

On the other hand, anxiety can be devastating for some people, interfering with their daily lives to a greater extent. Anxiety progresses when specific brain areas function unsuitably, resulting in a flow of improper or illogical behaviors. Anxiety conditions can be recognized when there is a longstanding concern like this. Anxiety conditions, such as panic illness or social anxiety syndrome, may require people's treatment to live normal, happy lives.

Until lately, scientists expected that the amygdala, a small-sized brain area, was the centre of fear and nervousness. According to reliable studies, animals like monkeys with amygdala injury were particularly tolerant in the face of terrifying stimuli. An overcharged amygdala was presumed to be the origin of unsuitable fear and nervousness in patients with anxiety syndrome.

We comprehend that anxiety results from continuing communication across numerous brain regions. A single portion of the brain does not produce nervousness. In its place, how we perceive exchanges trigger nervousness among many brain locations.

One clarification for how this works is that we split the brain into emotional and cognitive brains. The cognitive part is the frontal lobe, where all of our spirits and opinions come together as one consistent involvement. The amygdala, situated deep inside the brain, is part of the emotional part. According to the hypothesis, we only sense apprehension when signs from the emotional part control the cognitive part.

Flooding of Stress Hormones

When you are anxious, your body goes into the attentive mode, gesturing your brain to get ready for flight or fight mode. Your brain floods your nervous system with hormones like adrenaline and cortisol to help you fight whatever has made you nervous. These hormones alert your body that something frightening is about to occur. Their job is to support you in fighting danger. They attain this by improving your insights and speeding up your reflexes. When the danger has passed through, the concerning part of your nervous system takes control and relaxes you down in a non-anxious attitude. When you have nervousness, you may not be able to attain that sense of calmness. As an alternative, the flow of strain hormones forces your brain to issue even more stress until you are overwhelmed.

Your starting point level of nervousness may increase if extreme amounts of stress hormones overflow the brain recurrently. You could move forward from mild nervousness, which most of us deal with on a regular basis, to modest anxiety. Moderate nervousness is a little more severe and irresistible, and it makes you troubled and disturbed all of the time. If your brain endures being tremendously subtle to nervousness, your anxiety level may increase when you are powerless to contemplate correctly.

Difficult Decision Making

The influences between the amygdala and the prefrontal cortex (PFC) are deteriorated by anxiety. The prefrontal cortex should kick in and assist you in coming up with a rational, logical reaction when the amygdala warns the brain of danger.

It promises that you can examine data logically, make knowledgeable decisions, and support yourself in problem-solving. This part might be considered your brain's intelligent counselor. The prefrontal cortex answers realistically in non-anxious brains when the amygdala sends out apprehensions. In concerned brains, this process is not equivalent. The connection between the amygdala and the PFC is feeble when the amygdala warns the PFC of danger. Consequently, the rational problem-solving unit of the brain is calm, leading to illogical thinking and disordered conduct.

Remembering Unwanted Things

Your body is under a lot of pressure when you are anxious. The hippocampus, the share of the brain that supplies long-term and background memory, shrinks due to stress. It may become more stimulating for your brain to get a hold of memories as the hippocampus shrinks. Anxiety fools the hippocampus into trusting that anxiety-related reminiscences are harmless to save and recall. As a result, the few recollections you do hold will be those related to anxiety. To explain it another way, anxiety reprograms your nervous system to recall disappointment, threats, and hazards. Memories of achievement, triumph, and security, for example, are suppressed deep in the vault of your brain.

Hypersensitive to Threats

Nervousness can cause your brain to become oversensitive to threats. Your amygdala enlarges when you deal with nervousness consistently. It is a small-sized structure in the region of your brain that keeps control of sentiments and moods. It acts as a regulator in your brain, always skimming for dangers. When the amygdala perceives danger, it directs a signal to the hypothalamus, activating the fight or flight reply. The amygdala is a large and oversensitive structure in the anxious brain.

Consequently, it produces a lot of false apprehensions. It is the main reason why individuals with anxiety conditions are more expected to feel endangered than those who don't.

2.2 How to Map your Brain in Anxiety?

It has been discussed worldwide that anxiety can get better for us at any time. It is the body's instant reply to pressure, and it can be activated when you are required to make a sudden and important decision and to face certain daily life challenges with an open heart. Going through your life with an anxiety illness, on the other hand, might be a very diverse experience. People with anxiety syndromes often feel worried, scared, suspicious, and frightened, even in less demanding situations. Their lives are disturbed by these irresistible opinions, which can have a harmful effect on their professional and household lives. Luckily, research proposes that a method known as brain mapping could be able to decrease nervousness and reinstate the health of worried brains.

As the name implies, a brain map is a graphic representation of your brain. The image, occasionally called a QEEG (Quantitative Electroencephalogram), portrays how your brain does its job and permits you to see brain patterns that disclose mental strengths and inadequacies. Brain mapping is comparable to a brain suitability test because it reads and examines your brain's electrical action.

A cap is usually placed at the head of the patient under the brain scan. The mapping is done with the help of an advanced software program by taking electrical impulses. The latest technology is an extension of outdated EEG (Electroencephalogram) brain monitoring. In a nutshell, QEEG images measure brain action using conductors and head caps. The information from the brain waves is documented using specialist processers and treated using unique procedures that psychologists and doctors use to inspect the data for more careful results.

The results of brain plotting can be utilized to expose the central causes of illnesses, assess indications more evidently, and build treatment mechanisms that best encounter a client's requirements once they have been carefully analyzed. Physicians who need to comprehend how a client's brain performs at the nano-second level will benefit from such a mapping technique.

In simple words, brain mapping helps psychologists and doctors by letting them see where parts of their clients' brains are not functioning properly. Medical specialists can find trouble-making locations or upsetting behavior more evidently and appropriately than before by noticing electrical activity or watching the fundamental anatomy of the brain.

Medical experts can address diverse brain conditions and endorse specialized therapies, such as neurofeedback, therapy, medication, and other treatments after they have more comprehensive information.

Diverse types of brain scans can help treat nervousness and unhappiness because brain mapping develops precise two-dimensional and three-dimensional combinations of clients' brains. Medical employees can benefit from a better comprehension of patient brains by allowing the experts to:

Examine the motives of anxiety and despair, such as whether they are due to hormone issues or some other brain activity.

Check if the treatment substitutes over the drug remedies that are expected to be influential.

Inspect whether or not other conditions or situations are causing or growing their customers' nervousness or depression.

For many years, medical authorities struggled to understand the worry, hopelessness, and other neurological diseases. Considering the nature and the diversity of indications, it can be tough to precisely diagnose these conditions even today.

Nevertheless, brain mapping is helping us to change that perspective by allowing medical experts to deliver clients with individualized, accurate diagnoses and related services, even for threatening conditions like anxiety and depression.

Neurofeedback

It is a type of Neurotherapy and is most frequently known as Electroencephalogram EEG biofeedback. Neurofeedback is displaying info from thorough QEEG testing and scans to the patient. As the person undergoing Neurotherapy obtains a better comprehension of his or her brain activity, they or will be able to make mindful adjustments to their brainwave activity. In simpler words, the client will be able to "train their brain" for both short- and long-term respite.

Using such a technique, individuals are trained to use computerized biofeedback apparatus to treat their thought patterns or brain action problematic areas. Additionally, this sort of action is a non-invasive and submissive therapeutic method that can treat an extensive range of complications, together with anxiety, sadness, and cognitive inflexibility.

Nevertheless, such a technique does not fit well as a perfect diagnosing technique for all cognitive illnesses. Before trying to experience neurofeedback conduct, clients should speak with their healthcare experts, psychological specialists, or physicians.

A combination of factors or situations can bring on nervousness and despair. Hormonal inequities in the brain regularly cause these illnesses. Moreover, medication or lifestyle alterations can help to lessen their indications.

Medical specialists, for example, may use such a technique to tackle nervousness or unhappiness after conducting complete brain scans. Psychologists can train patients to adjust the way they think and regulate their brain's electrical patterns by using electrical images to notice how the brain responds when exposed to specific stimuli.

2.3 Brain & Panic Attacks

Panic is a defensive reaction to danger. While anyone of us can have a panic occurrence, a panic condition is categorized by the fear of different things. People with panic disorder frequently experience intense heart shivers, shortness of breath, dizziness, and a fear of having a heart attack. Physical indications produce anxiety or fear. Unexpected panic attacks might also turn into anticipated panic attacks. For example, after having an unforeseen panic incident on the train, the subway can become the trigger for a predictable panic attack.

Scientists are unceasingly researching the impacts of panic episodes on the brain. During such an incident, it is expected that the areas of the brain related to fear become more energetic. As per recent studies, people with panic disorder showed a lot of movement in a portion of their brain linked to the "fight or flight" reaction.

Other research has exposed reasonable associations between panic disorder and brain substances. It is also likely that the disease is related to a serotonin imbalance, which might damage your mood.

When people are nervous, their concerning nervous system goes into overuse mode, giving out energy and forcing the body to respond. The parasympathetic part of the brain then kicks in, bringing the body back to a more comfortable state. If this part of the system fails to function correctly, a person will remain energized and may experience sharp arousal related to a panic attack.

Researchers lately exposed that particular parts of the brain become overexcited during a panic occurrence. The amygdala, which is the brain's centre and midbrain areas that take control of various activities, including our awareness of pain, are among these positions. Functional MRI was utilized in research steered by scientists at the University College London to check which brain areas triggered when a person noticed an imminent threat. They detected activity in the region of the midbrain that activates protective responses.

Such studies can recall our understanding of anxiety-related diseases and, in turn, help investigators develop improved treatments by pinpointing brain areas involved in panic incidents.

When people are going through difficult emotions, such as nervousness or grief, they regularly seek advice and love from others. Social provision can be helpful to one's intellectual health, which is why it is so vital for people who are facing panic disorder indications.

It is usually related to social separation due to its nature. You can do things to be an accommodating friend if you have a loved one or associate who suffers from panic disorder. When a person is going through a panic attack, communal support can also be helpful. A powerful and overwhelming involvement might occur when someone has a terror attack.

Panic episodes are often misdiagnosed as a medical emergency, such as a heart attack. Before a person is appropriately recognized with this mental health problem, he or she may have to visit the emergency department numerous times. This can be upsetting for the person suffering from panic disorder and the family.

You must stay quiet and calm if you happen to be present during one of their panic attacks. It might be damaging to a person who is suffering from a panic attack if they have faith that you are frightened of them or annoyed with them. Out of all the available options, prefer keeping your cool and try to avoid joining them in a panic situation.

Endurance and faith are vital elements in assisting someone with a panic condition. When a person with such a disease or a condition is placed into a situation they aren't ready for, their anxieties can become overwhelming. The symptoms will only worsen by quickly poking them into a panic-inducing atmosphere or telling them that they are being overdramatic.

How can you Assist?

There are numerous actions you may do to assist people with panic disorder. Keep in mind that communal ties can play a major role in supporting an individual in surviving, so seek things you can do to help.

Getting maximum information about the panic condition is the best way to begin comprehending what someone with it is going through at the moment. It might make you feel more organized and knowledgeable.

While your closer one goes through this trouble, you must reserve your quality of life. Taking care of yourself in such situations and your significance can aid you to feel less angry. It does not matter what the other person is doing or what is he or she going through; the first thing is to not let them affect you in any way possible. Always stick to your plans.

Don't completely change your life to give space to someone else's anxiety. For example, if you had a plan to go out with your closest ones, you should still do it, even if they are scared to do so alongside you. Set limits with them, such as constraining the number of phone calls you will take while at work or choosing which days you will be available to support them outside the home.

If you want to help your friends and loved ones who are affected by such issues, you need to understand their issues first. Try to look out for a suitable time when you think they are behaving normally to listen to your point of view. Once you go through the issue in detail, only then will you be in a position to suggest some appropriate solutions.

Chapter 3: Mastering your Anxious Brain

Medical studies reveal that anxious thoughts can affect us greatly in our daily life routines. Our thinking process will be affected the most and we will not be able to perform our duties in a productive manner. Therefore, it is important to learn the techniques that can help you tackle such issues with ease. The following passage will give you much-needed insights in this regard.

3.1 Understanding the Anxiety Issue

Now and then, we all feel the effects of what we know as anxiety. This feeling is commonly referred to as "stress" at low levels, and it can be important to a certain life situation. Stress before an exam, for example, is common and helps to inspire focus, which is usually beneficial in such instances. However, there are instances when our inner reaction is more intense than the outward event to which it is tied, or we experience elevated amounts of agitation for unknown causes. So, if stress and anxiety are both variants of the same fundamental experience, how do we distinguish them apart?

In principle, you can determine this by examining how well the alternative interpretation reflects the internal reaction (e.g., do the emotions make sense in light of the scenario?) Consider how much your emotions affect your sense of well-being and capacity to complete tasks. If your inner restlessness interferes with your everyday life or feeling of well-being, especially for no apparent reason, you may be suffering anxiety levels that should be investigated. In reaction to a trigger, stress causes physical or mental tension.

Consider the following scenario: It is the final week of your semester, and you are unprepared for your exams. "I don't have time for studying for these finals!" you might think under stress. Anxiety would combine your stress with other anxieties, uncertainties, and expectations: "I will never be able to catch up on my study." I will be expelled from school and fail my finals, and everyone will think I am a failure." Different emotional and physical responses will result from these thoughts. Anxiety may cause you to sigh, reconsider your priorities, and intensify your learning efforts. Conversely, stress can reduce learning and a rise in non-productive activities such as excessive anxiety, substance abuse, eating disorders, and other non-productive diversions. Anxiety disorders do not go away when the extrinsic stressor is removed, and they may even cause new stressors.

Another scenario: You have been extremely busy at work and are beginning to feel stressed by the amount of work you have to complete. Stress causes you to think, "This is way too complicated for me to somehow get done today," It causes you to rethink your priorities and cross items off your to-do list, though it means having an awkward talk with a boss or boss coworker. If the stress progresses to clinical anxiety levels, you may begin to believe that "everyone is placing too much weight on me." However, if I do not complete this task, I will be dismissed. How would I pay my bills and insurance if I am fired?" Alternatively, you may feel so upset that you find it difficult to do anything on your to-do list and therefore can quit worrying about what might occur in the future.

One common sign of anxiety is irrational thoughts, which are agitated or otherwise troublesome opinions that become trapped in your head. Other anxiety-related psychological symptoms include being quickly annoyed and having difficulty concentrating. Physical symptoms of anxiety include headaches, muscle soreness, a racing heart, and difficulty sleeping. Anxiety can induce confusion, overwhelming anxiety, and an inability to comprehend or make smart decisions in severe cases, such as those discussed below.

Anxiety can be divided into three categories: thoughts, physical symptoms, and behaviors. They can be so intertwined and instinctive that it is impossible to distinguish them as distinct parts of a larger experience.

Our attention is drawn to the apparent threat when we are vulnerable. Because our minds have trouble distinguishing between something real and what is imagined, the threat could be genuine or nonexistent. We are on full alert as soon as we feel it to be harmful. What we think of ourselves in a circumstance shapes our view of it. Themes of hazard (physical, emotional, or social), danger, or susceptibility dominate anxiety-related thinking.

Our brain sees these thoughts as a warning to prepare for danger, resulting in a preoccupation with survival and trouble concentrating on everything else. Students worried about their grades have trouble concentrating on the test questions. People nervous in social circumstances find it difficult to understand a discussion. People who suffer from panic disorder are excitable of their bodily symptoms to the point where they can scarcely do anything but think about them.

When confronted with danger, our instinct is to flee. We normally feel relieved after escaping. We will strive to avoid situations that we believe to be risky in the future. When escape appears impossible (which could happen in a couple of moments), we may try to assault. Another option is to freeze (or act dead), hoping that the threat would disappear and forget about us.

The more nervous our thoughts become, the more extreme our physical reactions become, and the stronger our want to flee and be secure becomes. We will have more anxiety-related thoughts and try to avoid the issue if we have greater physical reactions. The more we try to flee or ensure safety, the more we associate specific situations with risk and danger (via our emotions), and our physical reactions will grow more extreme.

Each of the three anxiety factors influences the other two, creating a vicious cycle. The good thing is that because they interact so effectively, if we address one of the worry elements, some other two will begin to fade, potentially leading to more unwanted cycles.

Have you ever thought about the reason that causes this sensation? Fear is an emotion that everyone will have at some point. As uneasy as it can be at times, it is what protects us safe from harm, and it is a necessary emotion for survival. Consider an animal that does not flee when a predator approaches; this is not an evolutionary advantage. Fear is categorized as anxiety if it lasts for a long time or when the reaction is out of scale to the stress or risk and negatively impacts a patient's quality of life. Even though it is a normal response to risk, some people seek out this adrenalin regularly, for example, by viewing horror films.

The complex process by which our brain reacts to environmental stimulation and develops fear involves multiple neuronal circuits and areas of the brain.

The amygdala, an almond-shaped collection of nuclei deeply buried inside the temporal lobe, has been recognized as the centre of these processes. According to studies, the amygdala plays a critical role in humans' perception, expression, and feeling of fear. The central nuclei of the amygdala are among the most well-studied areas in the brain. They have roles in regulating cortisol release via the paraventricular centre of the brain. They also help enhance startle reaction via the brainstem and modify the nervous system via the lateral hypothalamus. Fear acquired responses such as fear-potentiated fright and freezing were eradicated in rats in a study. As a result, the amygdala's principal output in creating fear is assumed to be this region.

The hippocampus also collaborates with the prefrontal cortex, which is involved in high-level decision-making, to assist moderate the severity of the fear reaction. The hippocampus not only carries messages to the anterior pituitary and activates the ANS, but it also transmits messages to the frontal lobe, which evaluates the stress response. This aids in determining if the fear reaction is accurate or excessive, and it will signal the amygdala to reduce activity if the latter looks to be true.

Even though anxiety symptoms are regarded as typical responses, they may need medical treatment if symptoms continue and are out of proportion to environmental stimulation that can cause a fear reaction.

Anxiety is defined by emotions of tension, anxious thoughts, and bodily changes such as elevated blood pressure, as per the American Psychiatric Association. Anxiety disorder will develop if these signs become recurrent. Anxiety disorders are marked by persistent and debilitating dread and anxiety, or rejection of perceived risks, resulting from abnormalities in neural circuits that react to danger. For example, in phobia sufferers, a study discovered a gap between both the amygdala and frontal cortex, two brain areas critical for overriding or decreasing the fear reaction.

Anxiety disorders are typically treated with medication or psychotherapy, behavior modification, and antianxiety medication. With greater knowledge of the neuronal circuits that underpin the formation of anxiety and fear, more treatment options targeting specific parts of the brain where injury could lead to fear and anxiety disorders could be developed.

3.2 The Immediate Stress Response

The brain activates three key communication networks that control physical activities in response to stressful circumstances. Experiments with rodents, mice, and small animals like monkeys helped scientists better comprehend these complicated systems. Scientists then proved the effectiveness of these mechanisms on humans.

The active nervous system is the earliest of these systems, and it transmits signals to muscles so that together we can react to sensory input. For example, when people see a whale in the water, they may flee the beach as swiftly.

The nervous system, which is made up of parasympathetic and sympathetic branches, is the primary communication system. Each of these procedures has a distinct role to play in stress response. The sympathetic nerve relaxes the arteries delivering blood to the muscles, allowing more blood to be delivered and more capacity to work. The blood flow to the epidermis, kidneys and digestive system are lowered simultaneously. The hormone cortisol epinephrine, usually known as adrenaline, enters the bloodstream swiftly. Epinephrine's job is to put the brain in a generalized state of arousal to deal with the problem.

In contrast, once the source of stress has passed, the parasympathetic nerve helps regulate bodily activities and calm the body, keeping the body from staying in a condition of mobilization for too long. The disease can arise if these processes are left unregulated and mobilized. The calming part acts to mitigate the negative consequences of the emergency part's stress response.

The neuroendocrine network, which also supports the body's internal working, is the brain's third primary communication mechanism. Stress hormones pass through the bloodstream and promote the production of other hormones that affect body functions like metabolism and hormonal balance.

Whether physical, like impending work pressure, or emotional, like chronic fear about losing a job, a stressful scenario can set off a sequence of chronic stress that causes well-coordinated physical effects. A stressful event might cause your heart to race and your breathing to increase. Muscles stiffen up, and sweat drops form.

The "fight-or-flight" response allows people and other animals to respond faster to life-threatening situations because it has originated as a survival mechanism. The precisely designed yet close series of hormonal fluctuations and physical reactions aids in the fight or flight from danger. However, stressors that aren't life-threatening, like traffic congestion, job stress, and family problems, can allow the body to respond.

Investigators have got an insight not only into how and why these responses occur over time but also into the long-term consequences of chronic stress on well-being. Over time, the body takes its toll when the stress response is activated repeatedly. According to research, chronic stress has been linked to hypertension, the production of artery-clogging plaques, and brain alterations that may cause nervousness, despair, and addictions.

The amygdala, a part of the brain associated with emotional perception, sends a warning message to the hypothalamus when a traumatic event occurs. This brain segment acts as a control station, interacting with the human body via the nerve system so the person can fight or run.

The hypothalamus functions in a similar way to a command center. The nervous system regulates such automatic body systems as respiration, heart rate, metabolism, and the dilatation or contraction of important blood arteries. It rapidly connects these areas of the brain to the human body. The sympathetic system works similarly to a car's pedal. It activates the fight-or-flight reaction, which gives the body a rush of energy to react to a potential threat. The parasympathetic division is a brake mechanism. It encourages a "rest and digest" reaction, which helps the body relax after a stressful situation.

People are unaware of all these changes because they occur so quickly. The amygdala & hypothalamus initiate this sudden indicator even before the visual centres of the mind have had an opportunity to completely comprehend what is going on. That is why people can jump out of the way of an oncoming car without even realizing what they are doing.

The hypothalamus initiates the portion of the stress response known as the hypothalamic-pituitary-adrenal axis HPA after the initial spike of epinephrine diminishes. The hypothalamus, anterior pituitary, and adrenals make up this network.

Many individuals seem to be unable to discover a method of reducing stress. Chronically low stress activates the HPA axis, similar to a motor running at too fast a speed for too long. Over time, this impacts the body, contributing to the medical problems connected with chronic stress.

Chronic adrenaline surges can cause damage to the heart and arteries, raising heart rate and increasing the risk of a heart attack and stroke. An increase in cortisol causes physical changes that assist the body rebuild the energy supplies lost during the stress reaction. However, they unwittingly lead to visceral fat accumulation and weight gain. Cortisol, for instance, boosts appetite, making people desire to eat more than that to gain energy. It also promotes fat accumulation of underutilized nutrients.

The stress reaction is created to give someone a rush of excitement so you can efficiently fend off attackers or flee them. This aided our forefathers in staying secure in severe direct attacks.

Our threats are now less tangible and more related to our manner of living, a threat to our status, a productivity requirement, or any situation in which the pressures associated may surpass our ability to deal or need us to work on management. The stress response can harm us if it develops into a chronic state of strain and our stressor is activated and our body does not return to normal via muscle relaxation. It is also vital to keep in mind that the intensity of the stress reaction is related to the concentration of a potential threat instead of a real physical threat.

This explains why two people might have distinct stress levels in the same scenario; some detect a threat while others do not. People can lower the intensity of their stress reaction by telling themselves that the threat they see is not as imminent as they believe. This is tough, especially for individuals unaware that it is possible.

Also, when someone is unpleasant to us in a strong social scenario, we may experience higher levels of tension than when driving a vehicle in heavy traffic, where our odds of getting physically wounded are substantially higher. This is also why, even when there is no real physiological risk (and relatively little interpersonal danger), we might feel intimidated and feel our hands shake and sweaty. Our feet chilly as the adrenaline and circulation flow redirection take action. This also applies when we have poor childhood experiences that serve as stress factors later in adulthood when we fear being wounded predictably but aren't truly in danger.

3.3 Make Space for Positivity

Positive and negative energies are two ways to define an optimistic outlook on life. Negativity can negatively impact your health and contribute to a gloomy outlook. On the other hand, positive vibes can help people feel more optimistic, happy, and healthy.

Maintaining a positive energy level can have various mental and physical benefits. Changing your mindset and behavior to be more optimistic can help you:

Generating better self-talk is a key component of stress reduction. Optimistic thinkers are less stressed and manage it better. Stress reduction can have a cascade of positive outcomes on your health and life. People who think positively have a lower chance of dying and living longer.

Keeping a good attitude might help you recover from setbacks. By associating yourself with positivity in your life, you may assist yourself in keeping a positive mindset. Even if you don't complete all of your chores, the writing process of a to-do list offers productivity improvements. Our brains prefer the structure & shut down in chaotic situations. Write down all of the essential "to-dos" in order of importance on a piece of paper. You may then start planning your afternoons and even months from there.

Understanding your goals for a day when you wake up will help you feel less anxious right away. Because there is only so little time in the day, this physical activity also helps you assess what you can realistically do. Be practical and set reasonable goals for yourself.

Make your quality of life better despite how busy you are. People who eat well enough and exercise a lot are less prone to develop anxiety and depression, and physical benefits. Your brain requires them to thrive, and good mental health requires nourishment. Diet and psychological health are linked, according to research.

This self-care practice is especially beneficial for falling asleep at night. After all, that is when we begin to feel overwhelmed by all the tasks we still need to accomplish. The list goes on and on! Our minds may run and race till the alarm is set off, and we are fatigued but still have to return to work.

The best way to tackle anxiety and fear is to confront them. Ignoring our anxieties makes us anxious and inhibits us from going forward. However, be careful with yourself and only do what seems safe! If you see yourself becoming increasingly anxious, take a rest and notice or do something enjoyable or soothing. You might seek to discover your fear again later if it feels comfortable, having a break as necessary. If you are having trouble dealing with chronic concerns or anxiety on your own, remember that counselors can be quite helpful in working through coping mechanisms. Working with a therapist to provide a secure setting where you may face your anxiety and rebuild your recollections is especially vital if you have experienced trauma.

You can attempt mindfulness and meditation if your nervousness is lower. Simply sit quietly and pay attention to what is happening. Observe when fear or worry starts. Be curious if you can. Keep an eye on the anxiousness.

Consider how it makes you feel in your body. Take note of any related thoughts. See if you can just watch it; don't get caught up in the story or try to modify it. Take a pause when you need to focus on something neutral, such as your breath or your hands in your lap.

It is important to remember that if you are too stressed to be curious, it is best to take a break and come to your senses and notice the things in the room or go for a short stroll.

Fear makes us notice and recall unfavorable occurrences, reinforcing our perception that the environment is dangerous. We can attempt to modify this by consciously observing what optimistic joy we have when we come across someone we care about, the pleasure of a bright day, the beauty of nature, the pleasure of an adventure, and the humor in a scenario.

Fear has the power to disrupt our perceptions of reality. Those who have been through trauma may have also suffered significant losses, leading them to consider the value of their existence and understand the meaning of fear and how to improve it.

Whether we are dealing with anxiety or trauma, it is critical to reclaiming our sense of meaning. People who revert to healthy behaviors following trauma can find significance in the terrible event and establish a feeling of safety in the world, according to an 80-year study on the factors leading to longevity.

Anxiety can sometimes make us feel cut off from the rest of the world. The longevity mechanism also discovered that the quality of people's social interactions was one of the most important determinants of how long they lived after experiencing trauma.

This is due to a variety of factors. Relatives can assist us in assessing the threat realistically. We feel more confident in our ability to deal with problems when we have the help of others. Having a beloved one nearby also calms us down and decreases our fight or flight reaction.

Being in the wilderness lowers fear and anxiety while increasing good feelings, as evidenced by the growing field of evolution therapies. People have described their emotions when they see a beautiful nature scene using terms like peace, beauty, joy, hope, and vividness. Being in touch with nature improves people's mental well-being by lowering blood pressure and pulse rate and generating stress hormones, anxiety, and terror signals.

So, if you are struggling with emotions of nervousness, go for a run or walk in a park or green area. Physical activity, in addition to the calming effects of nature, will improve your mood.

According to research and personal testimonies, many people of racial, cultural, sexual, and gendered minority groups suffer increased levels of dread and anxiety due to separation and prejudice, which can include violence. Ego can be a powerfully healing practice for constantly under threat persons. That is because self-compassion also entails contemplating the shared pain of others to cure yourself like a loving friend.

Chapter 4: Self-Tackling of Anxiety

All of us may have heard about several techniques, therapies, and medications to handle anxiety and depression. However, the research shows that human beings can also tackle such problems independently. It is only possible with the help of a little more self-reflection and self-evaluation. This chapter will let you know about such simple steps that everyone can adopt to keep the anxiety issues to a minimum.

4.1 Set Your Ambitions

There is a prevalent trust that stress is related to ambition in today's social order. We boast about not having adequate time to do all of our responsibilities, staying up until late at night or getting up early morning, and all of this might be directly or indirectly related to being ambitious. The evidence is that you are not determined enough if you are not stressed enough. But is it likely to be both ambitious and gratified?

Many extremely ambitious people are interested in prospering by an inherent fear of failing. While concern and fear can inspire them to work better and progress in their professional careers, they can also cause stress.

It is imaginable to be pleased and thankful for what you have while also longing for the accomplishments you desire to make in the years to come. Mindfulness plans, such as keeping a thankfulness diary, can help you emphasize the current moment and decrease stress, letting you challenge the large tasks at hand.

Ambitious individuals tend to come up with strategies for the future. While having a dream and being advanced are both optimistic traits, continually living for the future can lead to augmented stress. Spend some time compelling yourself to emphasize the current moment. Running after challenges is great and gets your adrenaline propelling. Those hormones are flowing, but you won't be able to rejoice in your achievements today because you are continuously looking to do something even better.

Determination is invaluable, eternal, and very appreciated. It is something you can materialize for yourself. It is the pure wish to attain or prosper at something. It can help as a foundation of motivation. It can be harmonized with the fortitude to help you attain success in almost any attempt. Determined people are labeled as successful in life. They draw consideration to themselves and make the most of every opening. Likely, you do not feel satisfied in your life at some point.

While it is outstanding to have an enormous goal to work for, concentrating completely on the process might lead to unnecessary tension. Taking the time to recognize and rejoice in tiny triumphs will aid you in feeling less anxious about the future. If your goal is to grow your enterprise by 100%, a win can be going to an interacting event, meeting a few attentive people about what you do, and letting them know about your plan.

4.2 Eat Healthy & Exercise

Nourishment, workout, and stress can all influence your anxiety stages. According to research, one's nourishment, degree of fitness, and intensity of stress can all affect one's involvement with the panic condition and panic occurrences.

Contemplate making some routine modifications to help handle your nervousness if you are suffering from the indications of panic syndrome. Specific meals and substances have been related to an upsurge in anxiety levels. Research has also designated that the medicines can have a noteworthy impact on persons with panic syndrome, potentially deteriorating physical indications of fright and anxiety, growing the occurrence of panic attacks, and hindering decent sleep at night.

Your emotional and physical well-being may be exaggerated by stress. It is also regularly escorted by an upsurge in anxiousness. Regrettably, stress is a common issue that many of us tolerate daily. You may, nevertheless, obtain some effective stress managing assistances to help you cope with your unavoidable challenges.

Relaxation approaches are happenings that support the decrease of stress and the improvement of one's relaxation reply. These approaches are modest to learn and can be used abundant times per day. Deep breathing exercises, advanced muscle easing, and visualization are typical relaxation approaches for anxiety and panic.

Yoga can be a kind of stress release that includes these calming practices and the added assistance of muscular tension decrease and body consolidation. Yoga comprises workouts, breath rehearsal, and deliberation that can support you to feel more nonviolent and stronger. It might support you feeling more energized and less nervous if you have a panic condition or anxiety.

Caffeine is one of the most predominant food influences that may cause anxiety in people. Many people drink a cup of coffee in the morning to feel more attentive and interested. Caffeine, nevertheless, can aggravate panic and anxiety indications. It has been connected to panic incidents and increased feelings of nervousness and irritation. It is also known to underwrite frequent physical indications related to anxiety conditions.

Caffeine's undesirable effects may make you wish to remove it completely from your diet. If you want to cut down on such intake, start slowly and progressively decrease your intake. Taking out symptoms such as annoyances, impatience, and irritability can happen if caffeine is shortly detached.

Other ingredients, such as sugar and alcohol, have been exposed to consequences on temper and anxiety. Low energy, nervousness, and sleep problems can all be produced by these constituents.

Physical action can also help to decrease stress levels. Upholding a regular workout program has also been related to enhanced mood, augmented self-esteem, and amplified energy. Exercise's countless assistances can also support to comfort many of the indications of fear and anxiety.

Workout for panic and anxiety can help to decrease the body's physical response to anxiety. Exercise can perhaps support lowering the occurrence and intensity of panic attacks in some conditions. Exercise can also help dismiss physical and mental stress and decrease spirits of dread and apprehension.

4.3 Take on your Responsibilities

When you are overworked, underappreciated, or misjudged, your attention and emotions might be pulled in various guidelines. Try to prompt what is producing your anxiety and request others to give their opinions. Then make it clear how you want this specific divergence to be established. Keep your consideration on the facts of the state of affairs and stay in the present. Even if they seem relevant, now is usually not the utmost moment to bring up old complaints.

It will be informal to lash out your list of complaints when you feel anxious, but sinking anxiety is not about winning. It is all about making a choice. Avoid using expressively charged overstatements. Because "you" sound condemning, start your verdicts with "I" declarations. If you are concerned about an anxious reaction from a colleague, bring in an unbiased third party like an HR (Human Resource) representative.

To help you handle anxiety, many industries offer therapy through employee support programs or can attach you to public mental health properties. Though it may be terrifying to speak out about your anxiety, you become an example for others at work when you take responsibility for your health.

The whole office will make a profit if you grow stronger associations, improve communication, and ask for assistance. Anxiety will continuously be present in your everyday life to some extent, but it does not have to stop you from achieving good work and liking your job. Keep in mind that, while worry is an unfriendly emotion, it also delivers you with an opening to advance in your work. The more you lecture your concern at work rather than evading it or complaining about it, the more thoughtful the stressor must be to hit you off your game.

4.4 Be More Social

In specific social conditions, everyone becomes anxious. Nevertheless, if you get agonized over social anxiety syndrome, a routine state of affairs can be problematic. You may be more uncomfortable and frightened in social circumstances than people with low self-confidence.

In some social conditions, it is usual to feel anxious. Nevertheless, ordinary meetings with social anxiety syndrome generate great concern, uneasiness, and disgrace since you are frightened of being inspected or evaluated adversely by others.

Anxiety and worry lead to evasion in social anxiety syndrome, which can disturb your life. Unadorned stress can all exaggerate relations, daily practices, and other happenings.

Even though social anxiety syndrome is a longstanding mental health issue, psychotherapy and drugs can help you shape self-assurance and improve your aptitude to interconnect with others.

It can support you to feel more self-possessed if you plan for social circumstances that make you worried. You may feel obliged to avoid some circumstances because they bring you worry. In its place, struggle to plan for the future.

If you suffer from social anxiety syndrome, evading social circumstances can be alluring. Nevertheless, it is dangerous that you go out there. Accepting invitations to go to places and do things that make you uncomfortable is a good instance of this. At the same time, you must formulate yourself to deal with a situation while being out in the community.

Don't haste into big social meetings. Make plans to enjoy yourself with friends or family to keep your low-confidence issue at bay. Make a struggle to make eyes interact with outsiders on the streets. If somebody starts a discussion with you, ask about their hobbies or preferred travel destinations.

As you gain self-assurance, you can advance to progressively challenging workouts. Permit yourself to be persistent. Defeat social nervousness, which requires time and repetition of the whole process. You are not indebted to challenge your worst concerns directly. You can encourage greater concern if you get affected by things too early.

4.5 Say No to Procrastination

Many patients with anxiety-related diseases, such as panic conditions, fight with procrastination. Many indications of the panic syndrome, as well as normal concerned personality structures, might subsidize procrastination.

If you have an anxiety issue, you are more expected to struggle with perfectionism. Your requirement to be perfect could be contributive to your procrastination problems. Perfectionism may seem to be a helpful quality.

Setting such a high standard for yourself, on the other hand, can stop you from finalizing your responsibilities and lead to feelings of defeat. Likely, you are automatically retaining perfectionism as a method to put off doing your work.

Anxiety and procrastination are indistinguishably connected. When we are concerned about something, we tend to put it off. When you put off your driving license test because you are frightened of failing or getting upset while driving, or you are too anxious to ask out the person you have an infatuation for, this is occasionally clear to the person feeling it. The connection between apprehension and procrastination, on the other hand, isn't often understandable to patients or audiences.

People can be anxious about completing jobs they have a lot of know-how with, particularly if they are unable to complete a job in a specific period, the risks are advanced, or the assessment of their presentation will take a dissimilar form than it characteristically does.

When you are anxious about a task you have finished many times before, stop thinking about what's new this time. It can be problematic to notice when other feelings take superiority over anxiety. Another state of affairs is when you are angry about something you have to achieve that has nothing to do with a specific individual.

Perfectionism is a shared reply to anxiety among anxious people. When there's something they truly want to do right, they could generate jobs in uncommon ways. This can make a task that might be attainable if kept on a controllable scale feel completely irresistible, leading to procrastination. Nevertheless, the anxious individual regularly fails to notice that their method to a task is dangerous when associated with how other people would tackle it.

4.6 Get Closer to Nature

The experts suggest that going out in nature can help with anxiety, tension, and unhappiness. Innumerable studies have exposed that being in nature is good for your mental well-being. What you understand, perceive, and experience in nature can promptly lift your feelings.

There is a considerable link between spending quality time in nature and having fewer hostile feelings. Irritability, insomnia, tension annoyances, and indigestion are examples of anxiety, unhappiness, and psychosomatic disorders.

According to recent studies, our environments can upsurge or decrease our pressure levels, which affects our bodies. You may feel anxious, unhappy, or abandoned due to the strain of an unwanted environment. Consequently, your heart rate, blood pressure, and muscular strain rise, while your immune system is repressed. This is overturned in an enjoyable atmosphere.

Being in nature or viewing nature videos declines annoyance, terror, and tension while growing pleasant spirits. Nature not only recovers your expressive comfort, but it also advances your physical well-being by letting down common human diseases like blood pressure and heart issues.

Additionally, nature supports us in coping with uneasiness. We are indulged in the beauty of natural scenes and became unfocussed from our discomfort and suffering. We are hereditarily designed to get engrossed in fascinating natural elements.

This is recognized in a study of gallbladder operation patients, in which half had a view of plants and the other half had a view of a white wall. According to Robert Ulrich, the lead researcher, in this case, patients with a view of plants managed pain in a better way, seemed to have fewer negative influences, and consumed less time in the hospital. Comparable consequences have been shown in a more recent study using nature surroundings and plants in hospital rooms.

It does not matter if sleeping issues are bothering you. A two-hour walk daily is all it takes to recover sleep excellence and ease sleep issues.

The natural world can also tackle grief. Being in nature recovers handling skills, such as self-awareness, self-control, and patience.

Nature's helpful effects influence how you treat others. When people are exposed to diverse nature, they become kinder and more optimistic.

4.7 Have a Pet

There are numerous compensations for having pets in our daily life. Only lately have systematic studies begun to look into the assistance of human-animal collaboration.

Pets have progressed to be highly subtle to human behavior and sentiments. Dogs, for instance, can comprehend a lot of the words we say, but they are even better at understanding our tone of voice, gestures and body language. A trained dog will look into your eyes, just like any good human friend, to measure your expressive condition and understand what you are thinking and feeling.

Pets, chiefly dogs and cats, can help with strain, nervousness, and depression, as well as solitude, workout, and liveliness. They can also help with vascular health. It is vital to mention that taking care of an animal can help children become safer and livelier as they grow up. Pets are also a super source of companionship for senior people in society. But, maybe most prominently, a pet can provide you genuine pleasure and unqualified love.

While it is factual that people who have pets are inclined to have a better well-being than those who don't have any pets, a pet does not have to be a dog or a cat only. You can also have pets like rabbits as these will always give you a fuzzy, touching experience. Birds can help you uphold your mental perceptiveness if you are an adult.

Pets gratify the typical human wish for touch, which is one of the reasons for their therapeutic effects. Even the hardest criminals in prison validate long-term interactive developments after interacting with dogs, with many of them experiencing mutual friendliness for the first time. When worried or anxious, caressing or touching a loved animal can rapidly relax and comfort you. Solitude can be alleviated by having a pet, and most dogs are excellent stimulants for good workouts, which can significantly improve your mood and lessen sadness.

Pet possession benefits not just single persons but also complete families. Pet ownership may also teach youngsters the worth of life while also trusting them with some of the maintenance and nourishing responsibilities.

Taking your pets for a walk or run is an amusing and sustaining way to get good daily action. As per studies, dog owners are significantly more expected to meet their everyday activity necessities, and exercising every day is good for the animal. It will reinforce your bond, remove most behavior problems, and keep your companion fit and healthy.

Companionship can help you evade sickness and perhaps add years to your life, whereas loneliness and isolation can induce depressive symptoms. Taking extra care of an animal can make you feel desired and loved. It also helps in diverting your attention away from your troubles, which is especially beneficial if you live alone.

4.8 Follow a Routine

Some people relish having a reliable daily routine, while others hate the idea of following one. Upholding structure and consistency, on the other hand, might help you feel more organized and in control during periods of high stress.

Routines can be helpful at any time, especially if you are trying to create good conduct, but they are particularly vital when things in your life are unpredictable.

Lack of structure and orderliness can degrade spirits of anxiety and cause you to focus more on the root of your dilemmas. People who lack structure and have less emphasis are expected to worry about the problematic situation more, leading to additional stress and anxiety.

The impression is to create a pattern that gives your day order and expectedness. Of course, your timetable may vary dependent on the day of the week, but ensuing to a basic routine will help you feel less harassed and more organized.

Organizing your day guarantees that you do the essential duties that must be accomplished, leaving you time to schedule other happenings that you want or need to assume.

Upholding order and orderliness throughout your day will help you disrupt the design of deliberating based on your stress.

Making a list of the errands you frequently complete daily is one valuable activity. You can begin making a universal plan for what you might need to achieve each day to stay on track once you have an impression of the vital activities you need to complete.

While getting the basics done is vital, make time for things you appreciate, whether viewing a favorite show or calling a friend.

It is vital to sit down, recognize what is worrying you, and address your subjects if you are dealing with anxiety. Our bodies regulate and know what to imagine when we build regular practices through exercise or regulating our sleep patterns.

Chapter 5: Modern Techniques for Anxiety Removal

We may face anxiety issues in some parts of our life. People can feel prone to anxious thoughts during testing times of their life. The good news is that such a disorder is curable with the help of several therapies with the help of experts in the field. To know more about the possible therapies for removing anxious thinking, consider the options discussed in the lines below.

5.1 Cognitive Behavioral Therapy (CBT)

It is important to understand that you do not have to continue living with anxiety and fear, whether you are undergoing panic, obsessive feelings, incessant uncertainties, or a crippling dread. Treatment can contribute, and counseling is often the best operative choice for numerous anxiety matters. Unlike anxiety medicine, anxiety therapy addresses more than only the condition's symptoms. Treatment can aid you to find out what's causing your doubts and worries, help to relax, see proceedings in the novel in less frightening ways, and recover your managing and critical skills. Therapy explains to you the idea of using the skills you have been given to tackle anxiety.

Because anxiety syndromes are varied, treatment should be personalized to your unique symptoms and analysis. For instance, if you have obsessive-compulsive disorder, your treatment will be dissimilar if you need help with anxiety episodes. The period of your therapy will also be determined by the kind and extent of your anxiety problem. On the other hand, many anxiety treatments are only used for a shorter period. Different case studies show that many patients recover meaningfully after initial therapy sessions.

While numerous therapies are used to address anxiety, cognitive behavioral therapy (CBT) and exposure therapy are the most common. Each therapy can be utilized independently or in amalgamation with other therapies. Anxiety handling can be done individually or in a group setting with persons who have similar anxiety problems. The goal is to reduce nervousness, relax, concentrate, and overcome your doubts.

The most widely used therapy for anxiety syndromes is cognitive-behavioral therapy (CBT). It has been confirmed to be valuable in treating panic syndrome, fears, social anxiety conditions, and generalized anxiety syndrome, among other diseases. CBT is a type of therapy that focuses on classifying and redesigning problematic thought designs and behaviors. To put it another way, CBT can assist you in varying your approach to a state of affairs.

Feeling concerned or frightened is part of human life. Anxiety affects everyone to some degree at some point in their lives. Rather than the context itself, the way we think about a state of affairs often causes great worry, fear, or panic.

Creating space between a problem and your opinions, emotional state, and actions gives you the aptitude to handle it. It does not restrict you from attaining your goal or worsen the situation.

A lot of our daily-life experience is based on awareness. Having the ability to let go of ill ideas permits us to inspect various improved and more factual replacements, resulting in a better involvement and fewer simple uncomfortable emotions.

When you have disapproving feelings and ideas about a state of affairs, your behavior towards it can change over time. If a child has unfriendly sentiments about going to school, he or she may start making justifications not to go.

As time goes on, these conducts begin to duplicate themselves. You can study to consider those patterns and vigorously attempt to adapt them and the spirits that go along with them using CBT. It may be likely to prevent these behaviors from happening again.

CBT supports people in determining the links in the chain that lead to inferior anxiety and unhappiness: the unified thoughts, spirits, actions, and bodily sensations. The significant thing is that you may take steps for the discontinuity of the cycle of evading the anxiety-inducing situation.

Cognitive-behavioral treatment focuses on adapting automatic undesirable thinking that can aggravate emotional complications, sadness, and anxiety. These unreasonable negative ideas hurt one's mood.

CBT Techniques for Anxiety

CBT is far more than just recognizing thought processes; it spreads over various strategies to help people tackle them.

Role-playing, relaxation mechanisms, and mental disruptions are some of the methods used.

Recognize Negative Thoughts: It is all about learning how thoughts, sentiments, and state of affairs might help tackle maladaptive actions. The method can be thought-provoking, particularly for persons who have trouble with self-examination. Still, it can finally lead to self-discovery and visions, vital to the therapy process.

Learning New Skills

It is critical to start practicing new capabilities to be functional in real-life conditions. A person with a drug use syndrome, for instance, can start practicing new handling skills and practicing approaches to evade or deal with social circumstances that could lead to relapse.

Set Your Goals

Setting goals can be a cooperative tool in improving mental disease and making changes to recover your health and excellence in life. A therapist can support you with goal-setting techniques during CBT by coaching you to categorize your goal, distinguish between short- and longstanding goals, and emphasize procedure rather than the end outcome.

Problem-Solving

Learning problem-solving abilities can support you in classifying and resolving problems that happen from both big and small life burdens and dropping the negative influences of expressive and physical illness.

Self-Examination

Self-examination is a vital feature of CBT that involves keeping track of your activities, indications, and involvements over time and sharing them with your psychoanalyst. It can help your therapist get the info he or she needs to deliver you the best handling possible. Self-monitoring for those with eating illnesses can involve keeping a path of eating activities as well as any feelings or sensations that come with eating.

Challenging Thoughts

Thought challenging is about observing things from numerous viewpoints and using real-life instances. Instead of trusting that your judgments are the realities or not, thought challenging might help you examine things from a more impartial viewpoint.

Knowledge of cognitive misrepresentations can help a person identify when one is present in their judgments, letting them work to optimize the uncooperative views and substitute them with more composed and accurate thoughts.

You may have trouble rationalizing your problems if you come across anxiety. You may be concerned but have no impression why. On the other hand, you may have an unreasonable fear of anything, such as social congregations.

Activation of Behavior

If anxieties stop you from achieving something, you can plan it by writing it down on your timetable. It starts a tactic, so you don't have to keep getting upset about it.

For instance, if you are concerned about your kids getting sick at the playing field, plan a park hangout with a friend. This will inspire you to take action and address the state of affairs with the tools you have learned in CBT.

Journaling of Thoughts

Journaling is a method for getting in touch with and becoming conscious of one's opinions and spirits. It can also support you in establishing and illuminating your thoughts.

Make a list of the undesirable feelings and the good ones you can substitute them with. Your psychoanalyst may counsel you to keep a journal of the new attitudes and behaviors you practice between sessions.

No More Negative Thinking

There are helpful and unhelpful replies to a different state of affairs, which are characteristically decided by how you think about them. For instance, if your wedding has ended in separation, you may have faith that you have failed and cannot have another expressive relationship.

It may make you feel desperate, isolated, unhappy, and tired, and you may stop going out and meeting new people. You get trapped in a descending spiral, sitting at home unaided and feeling awful about yourself.

Otherwise, you can admit that many weddings end, learn from your blunders, and move on while staying confident about the future. This hopefulness can lead you to become more informally involved, such as registering in evening classes and making new friends.

This is a simple design of how certain thoughts, spirits, bodily feelings, and behaviors can trap you in a bad loop and even make new situations that make you feel inferior about yourself.

CBT pursues to break down the belongings that make you feel unfriendly, anxious, or terrified to disturb undesirable cycles like these. CBT can aid you in shifting your harmful thought outlines and boost your mood by making your complications more controllable.

5.2 Exposure Therapy

Exposure therapy is a type of behavioral therapy that is commonly used to help people suffering from phobias or anxiety disorders. It entails a person confronting their fears, whether imagined or real, in a secure atmosphere with the help of a qualified therapist. It has been proven successful and can be utilized with people of all ages.

Exposure therapy is a treatment that helps people overcome their fear of things, activities, or circumstances. Therapists and psychologists utilize it to address issues including Post-Traumatic Stress Disorder (PTSD) and phobias.

People tend to avoid things and situations that they are fearful of. According to the American Psychological Association, exposure therapy aims to help people overcome their fears by exposing them to distressing stimuli in a safe atmosphere.

Therapists utilize exposure therapy to help people overcome their fears and anxieties by interrupting the cycle of fear and avoidance. It works by exposing you to fear-inducing stimuli in a safe setting.

A person with social anxiety, for example, may avoid crowded places or parties. A therapist would identify the person to these types of social settings during exposure treatment to assist them in growing more comfortable in them.

For people with a Social Anxiety Disorder (SAD), exposure treatment can help them overcome their phobias of certain social and performance situations. Exposure training is usually done with the help of a therapist as part of a cognitive-behavioral treatment program, but it can also be done in your everyday life.

If you have social anxiety, you will most likely be terrified of these situations and avoid them entirely. This method can help you manage your anxiety in the long run.

While avoiding circumstances that you are afraid of may temporarily lessen your distress, you teach yourself that you cannot handle those triggers.

Leaving a situation in a panic also teaches you that it is something to be afraid of. Ideally, you should gradually expose yourself to increasingly uncomfortable situations and remain in them until your fear fades. This exposure training can be done in the real world (in vivo) or your head.

What does it Tackle?

Generalized Anxiety

Treatment for Generalized Anxiety Disorder (GAD) can entail both imaginal and in vivo exposure, albeit the latter is less usual. Compared to relaxation and non-directive therapy, Cognitive-Behavioral Therapy (CBT) and imaginal exposure enhanced overall functioning in patients with GAD.

Anxiety In Social Situations

For patients with social anxiety, in vivo exposure is commonly used. Going to a social scenario and not shunning certain activities are examples of this. According to a 2015 study reviewed Trusted Source above, exposure with or without cognitive treatment may be useful in lowering symptoms of social anxiety.

People with a fear of driving have benefited from virtual reality exposure therapy. It was useful in lowering driving anxiety in a short 2018 trial, although additional research on this specific phobia is needed. Other therapies may be required in addition to exposure therapy.

Speaking In Front of An Audience

Adults and teenagers have found virtual reality exposure therapy to be useful and therapeutic in treating public speaking anxiety. After a 3-hour session, participants' self-rated anxiety about public speaking decreased significantly, according to a modest 2020 study. Three months later, the outcomes remained the same.

Anxiety About Being Apart

One of the most common anxiety disorders in children is separation anxiety disorder. The most effective treatment is exposure therapy. This entails exposing the youngster to potentially frightening events while encouraging adaptive behavior and thought. The anxiety fades with time.

Exposure and Response Prevention (ERP) is a treatment for obsessive-compulsive disorder (OCD) that involves imaginal and in vivo exposure. Response prevention (not engaging in compulsive behaviors) is an aspect of in vivo exposures done in therapy sessions and assigned homework. Instead of engaging in anxiety-relieving practices, an individual allows the anxiety to subside independently. Imaginal exposure is utilized when in vivo exposure is too difficult or impracticable.

ERP is comparable to cognitive restructuring alone and ERP + cognitive restructuring, according to a 2015 research evaluation by Trusted Source. Exposure therapy for OCD is more effective when done with the help of a therapist rather than on one's own. It is also more beneficial when in vivo and imaginal exposure are combined, rather than just in vivo.

Anxiety Disorder

Panic disorder is commonly treated with interoceptive exposure therapy. Interoceptive exposure and face-to-face settings, meaning dealing with a trained professional, were connected with improved success rates. According to a 2018 research review by Trusted Source of 72 studies, people were more accepting of the treatment.

5.3 Dialectical Behavioral Therapy

DBT (Dialectical Behavioral Therapy) is a treatment that helps people deal with challenging emotions. DBT also teaches people to be present at the moment, manage their emotions, and healthily cope with stress. Naturally, researchers questioned if DBT could be used to treat those who suffer from severe anxiety. Fortunately, research shows that DBT can effectively treat anxiety, stress, restlessness, impatience, dread, and excessive concern.

Our ability to control and impact our emotions is emotional regulation. This can include altering our perceptions of unpleasant situations, lowering the strength of our emotions, or just distracting ourselves during a stressful situation. Anxiety sufferers have a difficult time controlling their emotions. As a result, many people who suffer from anxiety disorders get overwhelmed by their emotions. Fortunately, DBT can aid in emotional regulation. Individuals acquire two crucial skills in DBT: opposite action and self-relaxation

A variety of routes and therapy approaches can be used to direct the treatment process. Today's clinical techniques range from cognitive restructuring to rapid eye movement treatment, and they can address a growing array of mental health disorders.

What distinguishes one intervention from another? And more importantly, which one would most effectively and safely solve the challenges you are having?

While these questions might be tough to answer, the nature of your issue and any co-occurring mental health issues can help you figure out the best way to treat anxiety, sadness, and other mental health issues.

Understanding this method and its benefits for co-occurring illnesses can provide you with a lot of information about its benefits for your addiction.

Though DBT is best recognized for treating borderline personality disorder (BPD), it has a simple base. The concept of dialectics is utilized to promote both change and acceptance simultaneously. This permits patients to accept their current situation while also accepting that their future will have to change.

DBT is an empirically based treatment, which is supported by research. It consists of two primary components: skill development and individual therapy.

One mindfully indicates that fulness immersing oneself in the present moment can be a deceptively healing exercise. People frequently spend their lives obsessing about the past or the future. This can easily lead to anxiety as we meditate on what we have already done wrong or what we are sure to do wrong.

The notion is that by doing so, we will be better prepared to deal with future issues. This is referred to as a cognitive distortion.

Practice and planning are unquestionably essential. Constant concern, on the other hand, can be paralyzing. It can harm our psyches that productive acts become more difficult to recognize and carry out.

The truth is that immersing ourselves in the present permits us to better deal with future issues when they emerge.

This can be a strange concept in cultures, companies, and countries that function under the "work till you keel over" mentality. Self-care and maintenance are frequently ignored but crucial aspects of productivity.

It also helps to reduce anxiety by encouraging less ruminating on the past and allows us to deal with future challenges more efficiently from a more mentally grounded position. It aids in the prevention of burnout and its precursor, over-extension.

Self-Soothe

Self-soothing is a notion in DBT that relates to our ability to slow down emotional distress by focusing on physical cues. Taste, smell, sight, hearing, and touch are among the five senses.

This means practically limitless ways to apply this skill, depending on what works best for the individual. It can assist anxiety sufferers in "getting out of" their heads and re-engaging with the physical world.

One could, for example, take a bite of hard candy and assess how it feels and tastes. A favorite song or the gentle, relaxing feel of an animal's fur can also help them escape.

The activity can benefit anxiety sufferers because it temporarily substitutes rumination and concern. Taking a break from meditating allows you to think more detached and peacefully. This should allow the person to come up with more effective strategies to deal with whatever is causing their anxiety, or at the very least give them a break from it.

Fortunately, this technique can help you cope with both anticipatory anxiety and the aftermath of an emotionally arousing incident.

Radical Acceptance

It is one of the more difficult DBT skills to achieve since it requires more effort. It entails embracing the world as it is in the present moment. Doesn't it appear to be fairly simple? But what if you're dealing with a loved one's death, the end of a relationship, a humiliating job blunder, or a catastrophic error?

The idea behind radical acceptance is to accept that these painful experiences are real and true rather than avoiding them. As a result, mental energy should be directed toward accepting or changing the experience.

This can be life-changing for anxiety sufferers who focus on the why and how of the experience, meditating on their disbelief of the circumstances rather than how they will accept or escape the situation. Much anxiety stems from the belief that gaining a better understanding of the situation will change it somehow. This is frequently unintentionally false.

This is because rumination can be a preventative measure against being caught off guard by a problem or issue. It can, however, be used in clinically harmful ways. This can lead to people putting in enormous effort to see that their circumstances never seem to alter.

In DBT, the patient and therapist work in a team to resolve the deceptive contradiction between self-evaluation and variation to help the person in treatment make positive changes. Offering validation is a part of this process, making people more ready to collaborate and less expected to be distressed by the prospect of change.

In practice, the psychoanalyst authorizes that a person's actions look sensible in the context of their individual experiences without necessarily agreeing that they are the finest way to resolve a problem.

Although the structure and goals of each therapeutic setting differ, DBT characteristics can be found in group skills training, individual psychotherapy, and phone coaching.

Acceptance and change: You will discover techniques for accepting and tolerating your life circumstances, feelings, and yourself. You will also gain skills that will assist you in making positive adjustments in your conduct and communications with others.

Behavioral: You will learn to identify problems and detrimental behavior patterns, then substitute them with healthier and more productive ones.

Cognitive: You will concentrate on modifying ineffective or harmful attitudes and beliefs.

Collaboration: You will study how to successfully communicate and collaborate as a group (therapist, group therapist, psychiatrist).

Skill Sets: You will gain new talents by learning new skills.

Support: You will be supported to recognize and enhance your good strengths and attributes.

People can discover efficient strategies to control and express powerful emotions with this approach to therapy since it can help them improve their coping abilities. DBT is also beneficial regardless of a person's age, gender, identity, sexual orientation, or race/ethnicity, according to researchers.

DBT is beneficial in treating borderline personality disorder (BPD) and reducing the risk of suicide in people with BPD, according to studies. According to one study, more than 75% of persons with BPD no longer satisfied the diagnostic criteria for the disorder after one year of treatment.

For suicidal behavior, another study found that therapies that included skills training as a therapeutic component were more successful than DBT without skills training in reducing suicidality. While most DBT research has focused on its usefulness for persons with borderline personality disorder who have suicidal and self-harming thoughts, the therapy may also be effective for those with other mental health issues.

According to a study, this sort of therapy, for example, appears to be useful in treating Post Traumatic Stress Disorder PTSD, depression, and anxiety. DBT necessitates a large time commitment. People are required to do "homework" in addition to regular treatment sessions to work on skills outside of the individual, group, and phone counseling sessions. This could be a problem for persons who have trouble regularly keeping up with these assignments.

For some people, practicing some of the abilities can be difficult. People explore traumatic events and emotional distress at various stages of treatment, which can be painful.

5.4 Psychodynamic Therapy

Psychodynamic theory is the basis of psychotherapy for social anxiety, first attributed to Sigmund Freud.

As per the psychodynamic theory, social anxiety is part of a larger problem that begins in childhood. Anxiety is a childhood disorder, as per scientists who share this position. As a result, experts think your social anxiety arises from your early relationships with your parents and other important people in your life.

Psychoanalysis refers to the long rigorous psychotherapy, whereas psychotherapy is briefer. Psychodynamic treatment can be finished in as little as 15 days with once-weekly appointments, whereas psychoanalysis may require numerous weekly visits over several years.

In this way, psychodynamic therapy mimics cognitive-behavioral treatment (CBT) in terms of structure. Unlike psychotherapy, which needs a licensed psychoanalyst, psychodynamic therapy can be delivered by any therapist training in this area.

Psychotherapy for Seasonal Affective Disorder (SAD) aims to identify and address underlying conflicts that are believed to be the source of the disorder.

Your mental health professional will engage with you to uncover particular childhood conflicts and difficulties that may be related to your social phobia.

Moreover, your therapist will discuss any concerns about a social anxiety disorder that may occur throughout therapy. You might fear that your counselor will judge you, for example. You could also find it difficult to trust your therapist.

The awareness of suppressed emotions and unconscious variables that may be impacting current behavior is aided by psychodynamic treatment. People may act or react in certain ways for causes they are unaware of.

Psychodynamic treatment helps patients identify, bear and understand their feelings and emotions. It also educates students on being more adaptive and healthier in their expression.

People who receive psychodynamic treatment learn to recognize similarities in their connections and interaction. Without even realizing it, people develop different ways of responding to problems. On the other hand, learning to identify problems may assist people in coming up with new approaches to problems.

Emotional intelligence: Studies have demonstrated that psychodynamic treatment is beneficial in examining and analyzing emotions. As a result of increasing insight into emotional experiences, individuals can spot patterns that have led to disorders and make changes more easily.

A fundamental goal of psychoanalytic therapy is to improve social communication. Working with a counselor can help people understand how they frequently react to others.

The therapeutic alliance can be used to investigate a person's relationships with others through a process called transference. This allows people to explore and then adjust their response patterns in real-time to better their connections.

What is psychodynamic therapy's efficacy, and how does it contrast to other treatments?

Although determining the efficacy of psychological therapies is difficult, research suggests that they can help with various psychological problems. Many of the changes that psychodynamic treatment induces are difficult to define, making measuring its overall effectiveness difficult.

If you select psychodynamic therapy, you may visit your psychotherapist once or twice per week. You'll meet your counselor for several months, with each session lasting about 45 minutes. In rare cases, you may have lessons for another year or longer. During psychodynamic therapy, people are routinely invited to communicate about whatever is on their minds. This could be something they are going through at the moment now or recollections from the past.

It is a type of psychoanalytic therapy that focuses on achieving outcomes rapidly, typically in 25 to 30 appointments. In this type of treatment, people can choose a particular emotional zone to focus on. The patients meet with their psychologist at least weekly. They may seek counseling for months or even years. Psychoanalysts use a variety of techniques to get insight into your behavior.

Free connotation is a psychotherapist-led technique that inspires you to talk freely about your ideas with the psychoanalyst. This might bring you the development of unexpected memories and relationships.

Transference happens when you put your emotional state about another individual onto the therapist. You will communicate with someone as if they were the second individual after that. This technique can help your psychotherapist better comprehend how you connect with others.

The Benefits of Psychoanalysis

What sets psychoanalytic therapy apart from other procedures of treatment? According to an analysis of evidence comparing psychoanalytic techniques to CBT, the psychoanalytic approach has seven significant characteristics. It concentrates on emotions. CBT focuses on thought and behavior, but psychoanalysis examines the depth of feeling that a client is experiencing.

The concept of aversion is examined. People often try to avoid unpleasant feelings, thoughts, or occurrences. Realizing what a patient is attempting to avoid will help both the therapist and the client comprehend why this is occurring. Recurrent motifs have been discovered. Some people become conscious of their negative habits yet are powerless to change them. Similarly, others may completely be oblivious of their routines or how they affect their behavior.

We can have an idea by looking back at one's prior experiences. Other treatments tend to live in the moment, or how ideas and behaviors impact how people act. People can use the psychoanalytic method to learn more about their precedents and how they influence their current psychological issues. It has the potential to assist patients in breaking free from the chains of their past and living more completely in the present day.

The therapeutic association is highlighted. Because treatment is so private, the interaction between the therapist and the client delivers an exclusive chance to analyze and rewrite patterns of interaction in the treatment association.

Free-flowing is also one of the main benefits. Other treatments are sometimes quite organized, whereas psychoanalysis enables individuals to investigate freely. Individuals can talk to their doctors about their concerns, thoughts, requirements, and imaginings. Like any other method of psychiatric care, psychoanalytic therapy offers benefits and drawbacks. Before choosing this technique, it is vital to think about these factors.

The capacity to interact with possibly stressful or provoking situations is frequently required for success. While some opponents have questioned psychoanalytic treatment's efficacy, data demonstrates that extended and short psychodynamic approaches can help cure a wide range of disorders. Therapy that lasts longer than a year or around 50 appointments is referred to as "long-term psychoanalytic therapy." In contrast, short-term psychoanalytical treatment is known as a therapy that lasts less than 40 appointments or one year.

Symptoms are Lessened

Modest to large performance for decreasing symptoms of various diagnoses were identified in a study on the efficiency of long-term psychoanalytic treatment.

According to research published in 2021, short-term therapy led to long reductions in somatic signs, symptoms of depression, and panic disorder.

Long-Lasting Enhancements

People who have psychoanalytic handling are more likely to sustain these gains. The majority of the people recover even afterward in therapy.

All treatment options have possible disadvantages that should be evaluated. Repeated sessions are common in this sort of therapy. Traditional psychoanalysis can take 3-5 meetings a week for many years, whereas psychoanalytic therapy only takes one or two sessions per week. Therapy costs might easily pile up based on how long treatment lasts.

Counseling with a psychoanalyst can be taxing. It entails triggering emotional reactions while putting established security mechanisms to the test. While the procedure can be unpleasant at points, it can also make you realize the hidden forces that affect your current behavior.

5.5 Acceptance and Commitment Therapy

It is a style of psychotherapy that focuses on accepting negative ideas, feelings, signs, or situations. It also motivates you to commit to healthier, productive activities that align with your values or aspirations.

Theoretically, ACT therapists believe that growing acceptance might lead to greater emotion regulation. This process has several advantages, including the potential to help people stop suppressing particular ideas or emotional states that can lead to more issues.

Unlike Cognitive-Behavioral Therapy (CBT), the purpose of ACT is not to diminish the number and severity of negative internal experiences such as disturbing irrational beliefs, emotions, or cravings. Instead, the aim is to diminish or eliminate your battle to control or avoid these sensations while boosting participation in important life activities.

Your counselor will assist you in learning how to integrate these principles into your life during ACT. They could educate you on how to practice acceptance and intellectual cognitive restructuring, or they could assist you in developing a separate sense of self from your emotions and feelings.

Mindfulness activities can also be used during sessions to promote non - judgmental, healthy attention to thoughts, emotions, sensations, and recollections that you might otherwise avoid. Your counselor may also assist you in identifying times when your behavior did not align with your beliefs, as well as assisting you in determining which behaviors would be appropriate.

Your therapist may offer homework, such as meditation, cognitive, or values clarifying activities, between sessions. You and your psychiatrist decide on the homework, which can be tailored to be as personalized and beneficial as possible.

Third-wave treatments were once thought to be especially useful for those who had failed to respond to previous treatments such as classical CBT. Nevertheless, it is currently thought that third-wave treatment may be appropriate as first-line therapy for some people.

According to research, the ACT is suitable for various diseases, including those that transcend multiple diagnoses. ACT tends to enhance people's standard of living and may help them cope with physical ailments and chronic pain. While ACT is a successful treatment for various disorders, research suggests that it may be on par with other forms of treatment, such as CBT. This data shows that somebody who responds well to ACT may also respond well to another therapy.

ACT has also been chastised for being too similar to other types of therapy. Some CBT proponents argue that ACT, like some other third-wave therapies, isn't a big departure from CBT. ACT may be provided by a psychiatrist, psychologist, social services, or mental health counselors, among other mental health professionals. If you want to learn more about this method, you can inquire about your therapy provider's expertise or look for an expert ACT practitioner.

ACT sessions are typically hands-on, with mental exercises or guided meditation and assignments following the session.

Completing these activities is a crucial element of ACT since it allows you to learn new abilities and increase your psychological flexibility. Your therapist will want to talk about your goals and values during therapy. This is an important element of a treatment since your beliefs will guide your activities in the future.

The Relational Frame Theory, founded on the premise that the human ability to relate is the core of language and cognition, underpins Acceptance and Commitment Therapy. Noting the boundaries along which a relationship exists is part of relating. We may identify apples with oranges, but our capacity to relate allows us to recognize that and they have a strong similarity (round) and purpose (to be eaten); their colors and textures are vastly different.

Unlike many other creatures, humans have an extraordinary capacity to link seemingly unconnected events, words, and concepts. While this is a useful skill, it also makes negative ideas and judgments about ourselves easier. If we can associate the term "cookie" with eating cookies, we can associate the word "worthless" with the sensation of being worthless.

For instance, we might associate the phrase "worthless" with my capacity to execute my job, therefore, by consequence, with my life. Relational Frame Theory is the foundation of ACT. We often develop relational connections that aren't complementary or life-giving. Still, when we use awareness to embrace our feelings and adjust how we react and interact with them rather than seeking to evade them, we may modify those relationships.

Chapter 6: Rewiring your Brain with Positivity

For the rewiring of the brain, the amygdala must have had specific experiences. To rewire your brain's emotional memories, you must expose yourself to the specific sights, sounds, and other stimuli that trigger your fear. The amygdala's reactions may be altered by activating these circuits, which generate the possibility for new connections between neurons. To form these connections, you must once again stimulate the neurons. To overcome fear or worry, you must first feel it. To get back on the horse that tossed you is more than just cowboy knowledge.

6.1 Engage in More Social Experiences

Being more social isn't about trying to please everyone. After a busy week, there's nothing wrong with relaxing at home and binge-watching your favorite show.

Getting yourselves out there can take many forms for different people. Maybe it is just hanging out with your closest friends or chatting up the delivery man for you.

Interaction, compassion, relational, and listening abilities are valuable in your private and work life. These abilities can be useful for employee engagement, planning, and teamwork. Let us look at what social skills exist, how to use them in the job and daily life, and why they are important in rewiring your brain with positivity.

Since social skills can encompass a wide range of abilities, it is critical to hone these skills, especially at work. For example, effective communication skills are vital in employment that need regular interaction with people and consumers, which encompasses the majority of occupations. Even if your profession does not require you to interact with customers, you will almost certainly need to interact with your coworkers, bosses, and other employees to execute your job well. Here are some of the most in-demand interpersonal skills in the workplace that will help your brain think positively and keep you away from negative thoughts.

empathy is essential for interacting with one another and discovering mutual interests. Empathy also permits us to truly comprehend the emotions, ideas, and opinions of others. It can be useful for team initiatives at work. You are far more willing and able to cooperate effectively and find great workplace alternatives when you better understand colleagues' viewpoints, appreciate their thoughts, and feel comfortable sharing your input.

Personality Traits

Understanding how to successfully communicate with people can allow you to interact in work discussions, spot and understand social cues–such as reading your coworker's present mood–and find ways of understanding others' characters to help you create relationships in the workplace. Better working relationships lead to increased prospects for advancement.

Interpersonal Abilities

Intrapersonal skills refer to comprehending your thoughts, feelings, and ideas. Intrapersonal abilities include:

- Communicating oneself in suitable ways.
- Understanding when to voice your opinions in professional contexts.
- Setting social limits and objectives for yourself.

For example, you could learn and practice tactics for productively engaging with a hostile colleague or developing and presenting creative projects in team meetings.

Ability to Communicate

Language skills such as attentive learning, writing, and nonverbal skills may be required in your field. If you work with consumers, you may want to acquire and practice effective listening skills to assist them in solving problems. If you are leading a team, you might want to study and implement tactics for increasing the efficiency and transparency of your team's mail and web conference communications.

Strengthening your social skills will help you in any situation. Social skills are crucial since they can aid in more effective interaction. Consequently, you will be able to form, establish, and strengthen stronger bonds with coworkers, customers, and new connections.

1. Participate in Group Activities.

Use open-ended inquiries to continue communication with people, family, and colleagues. Set a little goal for yourself during your next staff meeting to present at minimum one project or company strategy.

2. Begin with Little Steps.

Begin by engaging people you encounter on everyday life basis to improve your interpersonal skills. When a shop assistant asks about your requirements, you might respond with an inquiry about their day rather than a one-word reply if you are out purchasing. Likewise, you can seek ways to extend talks with friends or practice your communication abilities with long-distance relations with whom you don't speak as regularly.

3. Pay Attention to Your Employees' Social Abilities.

Observing your coworkers is another way to improve your social skills. Keep an eye out for nonverbal cues, body language (such as laughing and nodding), and their terminology to start a conversation. Examine what made your employees' interpersonal skills so efficient and effective. These findings can be referred to and incorporated into your language skills.

4. Improve Your Listening Abilities

Being an engaged listener is just as vital as also being able to contribute your own opinions. As a result, others will feel free to contribute their thoughts and ideas. Make eye contact while listening and use nonverbal communication such as nods when you approve or ask questions for clarity when you hear anything you don't grasp.

5. Take A Coworker Out to Lunch

Building relationships with people might be scary, but it is best to start small and focus on one person at a time. First, select a coworker in a similar position to you and ask them for dinner or coffee together. Having a common function or job obligations can provide conversation starters, but ultimately, try asking questions and learn about them as an individual. Engage on yet another level with people who work in various organizations as you create additional connections. This can allow you to expand your networking opportunities and better understand how your work affects the overall organization.

6. Be Open to Sincere Praise.

Praising others for a work well done is an excellent approach to showing warmth and gratitude. Be genuine; a false appreciation can backfire against you.

More Acts of Kindness

Let's face it: we have little influence over much of what occurs during the day. We do not influence how other people drive, say, and how much they expect of us, but we have authority over what we are doing, both in reaction to others and our initiative. If we want greater optimism in our lives, we must choose it, which isn't as difficult as we might think.

Having a more satisfying life begins with modest, simple actions that, when repeated, build up to a lot of happiness. Offering kindness to others has a multiplier effect: it pleasures their lives and yours.

It is not a large act, such as establishing a charity or contributing thousands of dollars. Rather, there are numerous tiny acts of kindness that you may perform on a routine basis to bring optimism into your life.

Please Express Your Gratitude

Everyone seemed to be preoccupied. We all contribute significantly. And we have all encountered those who took us for granted. It could be an employer, a partner, or a friend; chances are, everybody you encounter does something in their life that they don't feel valued for. You have the chance to appreciate them for anything, and a simple "thank you" may signify more to them than you realize.

Offer To Assist

This might take all day, such as assisting a buddy with moving to a new place, or it could only take a moment or two. Step in the next time you observe someone suffering from a small activity, such as sorting documents, reaching something on a high shelf, rising off the floor, cleaning up a spill, or moving an unusually sized or formed item. It will take a second to connect with another human, and the work will move far more quickly and easily for that individual.

Allow For the Possibility of Error

You can practice kindness by giving somebody the advantage of the doubt when they snap at you, knock you off in traffic, or take the last brownie. Perhaps his dog died suddenly and he is having trouble concentrating coherently. Perhaps she is rushing to go home to her ill child and isn't watching the road as much as she should. Perhaps he hasn't consumed anything all day!

Since the same person commits the same offense repeatedly, you may have to reevaluate your strategy and whether that person is testing your limits. If it is a one-time encounter with a stranger, giving them the benefit of the doubt is nice and liberating. It also allows them more time to reflect. If the discussion continues in a bad direction, that individual may feel vindicated in their actions. When you reply with compassion, the other person has a better chance of reflecting on his or her unkind actions and, maybe, choosing to act each time differently.

Consider whether you found yourself in those circumstances and acted with compassion after the day. You can tackle this without judgment or self-criticism: you may spend weeks without encountering a stressed parent to someone you can surrender your spot in line. You may occasionally see that frantic parent, but you, too, are frantic and harried, and you cannot give up your spot. That does not imply you are not a good person. That means you are treating yourself with kindness and respecting your limits. That is also a beneficial practice.

You can use your notebook to reflect on other person's good deeds and how they probably make you feel. Try to remember every detail of the moment and repeat the warm sensation in your memory as among the happiest times of your day. It could be an expression of gratitude you want to do for somebody else or one of your objectives for tomorrow.

A Friends Day Out

Surrounding oneself with positivity and leading a more positive mindset appears simple. However, negative factors can sometimes trap us due to circumstances beyond our control. Stepping back from relationships that may have deteriorated since we initially entered them, or removing oneself from an entire network of friends, can be difficult. Friendships and connections can assist (or hinder) our mental health. Therefore, it is critical to surround oneself with optimism. Because well-being is key to reaching our ability and making sound judgments, it is critical to pay close attention to our mental well-being.

Establishing a support system can help you be more accountable, boost your emotional and physical health, improve your problem-solving abilities, and improve mental fitness. Being held responsible for whatever you do is important in achieving and maintaining healthy lifestyle changes. However, transparency is most effective when it is shared. We must enable our support network to communicate their accomplishment when we submit our success to somebody else. Social programs have also been good for sustaining emotional and physical health and preventing psychosocial disorders like anxiety and cardiac problems.

They can improve problem-solving abilities and mental flexibility even while reducing stress.

Interacting with people can help us maintain mental sharpness. So, we need to figure out a practical strategy to increase our good circles, reduce our negative ones, and surround ourselves with individuals who want us to succeed.

Reaching out is difficult, but it is necessary for rehabilitation and treatment. This does not imply that people must tell everybody in their lives about their mental struggles. Patients can share whatever information they choose with people with similar interests. First and foremost, we must examine what we choose in our support system. These will most likely be the folks we observe in their everyday lives as being nonjudgmental and compassionate; this promises well enough for their support in our lives. Don't forget about the professionals. Many people ignore that psychiatrists can also be regarded as beneficial support systems while forming their networks.

We should explore contacting any adherence to standards that can assist us in accomplishing our objectives. Others who can help us examine are those in our professional circles. Many of us may struggle with this one. It is never simple to decide to choose whether or not to tell employees about our sicknesses and treatments. Although the psychological state is now far more widely recognized and understood than in earlier years, there is still some social stigma. Communicating with a specialist can assist you in choosing to speak with colleagues. During tough times, a great support system can assist patients in finding the correct balance in life. We are social creatures with brains designed for social connection and participation in the lives of others. Joining groups based on interests, donating, taking a course, or expanding community engagement are excellent ways to sow the seeds of support networks.

Be Ready to Help

When there is a disagreement, we either join together and unite as a family, group, or nation or break apart and scatter into our cocoons.

That won't work and we need one another in difficult times. We cannot continue to isolate ourselves from one another and insult the suffering of others. The ability to interact and empathize with one another is unique to the human race, particularly during difficult times.

We must help one another as there will be times when you need me and when I need you. We all need aid, despite how good we are.

All we like doing sometimes is crying on someone's shoulder. In other instances, we face seemingly insurmountable challenges and require the assistance of others to speak them through and clarify them in our brains.

There is no greater method to demonstrate than to lead by example. People will notice when you become a happier person without you saying anything. Suddenly, instead of blue, gloomy, and dismal updates, your Facebook postings are about positivity and light. When they are around you, you often smile on their faces, and when something bad is happening, you find a way to make it positive.

Inspire your loved ones and friends to learn new things, congratulate them when they succeed, and demonstrate that they can achieve whatever they set their minds to. You think more favorably about diverse scenarios when you are comfortable and empowered well about yourself.

Appreciation is helpful not only to you but also to everyone else in your life. Begin to teach others when you are appreciative of something. Let people know how much you value and cherish their presence in your life.

Tell them explicitly what you enjoy and how it has influenced your life. Demonstrate by assisting them and being available to them in the same manner, they were to you.

Show somebody in your life how to become more optimistic if they seem depressed or overly pessimistic. Let them understand how you changed your perspective, found the bright side of any scenario, and turned it around for the better.

In the worst-case scenarios, simply being around them and assisting them in moving on is the greatest thing that can assist them in finding a positive spin.

Seeing the excellent traits in others might help you see your positive attributes. Gratitude may increase your joy and change your mindset. Gratitude is extremely beneficial in the workplace since it promotes peer regard, confidence, and admiration. Praising coworkers and performing small acts of kindness can help to spread gratitude.

Remember that words have tremendous power. Using phrases that are filled with positivity is known as positive communication. Your listeners' perception of your comments will change if you communicate in a good and constructive way. Personal, motivating, enthusiastic, and inspiring communication is essential. Furthermore, a good outlook will always be more effective.

Make it a daily habit to praise somebody for their hard work, but try to be sincere. Learning to recognize when you feel grateful is a part of practicing thanksgiving.

6.2 Get Some Fun Time

Sports

Sports have this incredible, one-of-a-kind ability to positively affect society. Sports make an impact every day, benefiting children, communities, and even nations.

Sure, nothing is perfect, although there is good that can be done using athletics as a platform. Major events benefit the regional economy, and kids are inspired to go and get active through the efforts of squad and player foundations.

So, instead of concentrating on off-the-field controversies or even during the matches, let's focus on the positives for a few moments.

Your behavior at sporting events has a significant effect on the children. How you behave, talk, sound, and participate on the sideline determines if you have a favorable or negative effect.

Your tone of voice and body expression significantly impact your child. It might take all the fun out of sports if your child believes you are angry with her after hitting a shot. If your child believes she is not excellent at sports, it can impair her self-esteem.

However, if you appear and sound like you are having a great time, your youngster will feel the same way. You could even tell your youngster how much pleasure you had seen him or his play as a team just at the end of the match.

Sports benefit the patient and provide additional benefits. You may appreciate sports since it allows you to spend some time with your pals. Perhaps you enjoy sports since they keep you in shape. Sports are also helpful for your mental wellness. You become calmer or less stressed after playing them.

Sports can help you relax, build muscle, and improve your health. It is easy to begin taking part in sports and reaping these benefits.

Stress-related illnesses account for 75 percent to 90 percent of doctor visits. Sports can help you cope with stress. Endorphins, the compounds in your brain that reduce tension, are released when you exercise.

According to studies, up to 20 minutes of activity, every day can help people relax. This tranquility lasts for several hours after the workout.

Golfing or skiing, for example, requires you to put your troubles aside and focus on the work at hand. This helps you relax and cleanse your mind. It also aids in better sleep.

Participating in team sports has a bigger influence on psychological health than participating in solitary sports. According to Australian researchers, women who play sports and basketball in clubs have better health than others who exercise alone, such as walking or hitting the gym.

Sports can help you overcome depression. Exercise has been shown in studies to relieve depression and lower the likelihood of relapsing. In one trial, the movement was very effective as normal antidepressant therapy, with even small quantities of exercise helping reduce depression.

Art Work

You might be shocked to learn that arts and healthcare have a long history of collaboration. Visual art, creative writing, role-playing, and theatre have been employed in institutions, mental health care centers, elder care homes, emergency departments, health professional clinics, pediatric care, and other settings for years to enrich personal experiences. People engage in creative projects whenever they are in a crisis, whether health-related or not.

Over time, the advantages of creative work have become widely acknowledged as just being "good" for people. Most healthcare providers intuitively understand that art makes people happy and feel a little better, particularly when at their lowest. While most individuals intuitively understand the need to incorporate creative activities into a healthy environment, the advantages were not explicitly defined or stated. As a result, the fine activities have taken up a range of positions on the outskirts of the health care industries.

Self-expression is a fundamental human need that everyone has experienced at some point. You don't have to go to art school, make marble sculptures, or have a natural talent for painting realistically; everything you produce is an expression of yourself, and it is lovely.

Art and artistic expression are important tools that can help you improve both your health and well-being.

Living a stress-inducing lifestyle can hurt one's personal health over life, and discharging pent-up tension via the process of art is a terrific way to relieve it. Drawing, sketching, clay carving, and photography are just a few examples of stress-relieving pastimes. Creating art necessitates attention and focus on the work at issue. You may become involved in the process, giving a mental break from the constant barrage of ideas and to-do checklists that plague today's busy mind.

Making art regularly is a terrific method to consistently reduce stress, leading to better mental and physical health.

Practicing and mastering an art may help you build creativity and utilize your entire brain. Although practicing creative skills and connecting with the imagination are not confined to art, they can be closely concerned with creating art. There is nothing right or wrong when it comes to art, and developing innovative thinking enables you to emerge with different ideas and plans at the moment. This thinking can then be applied to your daily life, infusing creative thinking into your latest work project or school homework assignment.

6.3 Trading of Negativity with Positivity

It should be clear that it is all about bringing positive thought processes into your life. Such a habit will help you tackle all the anxious thoughts and depressing moments. So, the need is to keep the negativity to a minimum while focusing all of your attention on positivity with the help of certain daily life practices. A few of these are discussed in the passage below.

Face your Fears

A person's amygdala often does not get the necessary learning experiences when left to its thinking process. As a result, the anxiety reaction may frequently thwart the process of effective exposure. An elderly woman who is afraid of flying may be able to see her family hundreds of miles away if she gets an airplane ticket as a present. As she prepares for the journey or arrives at the airport to board the aircraft, her nervousness rises. Her anxiousness, however, implies that she is in the ideal position to rewire the active circuits and adjust her amygdala's reaction to the circumstance. She does not recognize this. Rather than confronting her fear head-on, she will likely attempt to avoid the trip altogether. There's a chance she will come around or reason with herself if you try to persuade her that flying is safer than driving. On the other hand, her amygdala is not responding to stress based on logic; rather, it is about activating connections already in place.

When confronted with a dreadful scenario, a person's want to flee becomes insatiable. However, if that grandma refuses to fly, she will lose out on exposure and quality family time. Anxiety responses are difficult to change because of the cycle of feeling anxiety and then fleeing it by avoiding the circumstance. Anxiety may become self-perpetuating in this manner.

The term "activate to produce" might help you recall why you need to be anxious. This is necessary for amygdala learning to take place. Exposure-based therapy's success is predicated on the activation of neurons. To make new connections, turn on the circuits in your brain that hold memories of the dreaded thing or circumstance. Anxiety and emotional arousal indicate that you have activated the proper circuits. According to research, those with greater emotional arousal gain the most from early exposure. Systematic desensitization may take longer than flooding, accounting for ineffectiveness differences.

Exposure, encountering an anxious event or item while nothing terrible occurs, seems to enable another part of the brain to influence how the amygdala responds, according to animal studies and brain imaging. In the brain's frontal lobes, a region known as the ventral medial prefrontal cortex plays a role. Amygdala learning and memory storage occur upon exposure, with the amygdala storing the memories. The amygdala does not eliminate the fear learned and stored there, but new circuits and calmer reactions are learned.

Although it is unpleasant, engaging the circuitry of anxiety might help you recall how critical it is. If you want a nicer cup of tea, use hot water while brewing it. Coldwater will not enable the taste of the tea to be incorporated into the water if you put tea leaves or a teabag in it. In the same manner, new connections are formed when the neuronal circuits in your brain are engaged (or heated). If you want to rebuild your brain circuitry to combat anxiety, you must be exposed to heat.

Diagramming as a Tool for Exposure Learning

As an analogy, think about a small child scratched by a cat as an example. The scratch, a negative occurrence that produced pain, is linked to the cat, a neutral item that became a trigger. The upshot of this is that cats have come to induce fear. After this, he becomes anxious about animals and loses interest in playing with them, like cats.

We must retrain his amygdala by exposing him to friendly cats if we want to help him develop new circuitry and overcome his fear of them. His amygdala may be activated to develop new circuitry connected to cats when he sees or touches one under favorable conditions (while caressing it and appreciating its softness, being amused by its tricks, etc.). In the absence of unpleasant experiences, the child's new neutral or positive relationships with cats will become stronger, and he will have less anxiety. The child's amygdala will bypass his fear and anxiety with frequent exposure to friendly cats.

A fearful reaction to the cat is expected throughout the exposure. However, we need to expose the neurons to this stimulus to reorganize the neurons. The amygdala must be exposed to fresh encounters with a cat to modify the circuits it has established in the lateral nucleus. On the contrary, a child's nervousness signifies that the amygdala is engaged and ready to receive new information.

Changing the Way, You Think

The foundation of cognitive therapy is that certain thoughts are irrational or harmful, and they may lead to or worsen problematic patterns of behavior or mental states. Cognitive therapists ' primary focus is on ideas that cause anxiety or sadness and who are trained to detect and change these thoughts. Cognitive reorganization is the name given to this kind of problem-solving. Restructuring one's thinking to deal with worry affects the brain's cortex. You have probably heard of cognitive therapy if you have ever had self-defeating or unhelpful ideas. Every time we try to alter our ideas, we're attempting to alter the brain. Rather than being the outcome of brain chemical and neurological processes, our ideas are those very processes. Using your ideas to reorganize your brain is called cognitive restructuring.

As you have come to understand, the brain's dread and anxiety-inducing processes don't always need the participation of the cortex. As it turns out, fear reactions may be activated before the cortex has had time to comprehend them. Thoughts and interpretations are important, but this does not imply that they don't matter. They have an effect without a doubt. It's critical to know how thoughts influence the amygdala's responses and how their impact is restricted if you want to use this knowledge effectively.

Calming the Cortex

Activating the amygdala and causing anxiety may be done by thinking about and focusing on particular ideas and pictures in your brain. Because of this, it is possible to tell the difference between what one thinks about events and what happens. The mere act of imagining or contemplating something does not guarantee that it will occur. Your amygdala may not be able to tell the difference between your ideas and reality, so it is important to keep this distinction in mind. So, keep it at the forefront of your brain to inhibit your amygdala from reacting to imagined ideas and pictures with an anxious reaction!

Fusion of the Mind

When you know the distinction between your ideas about events and the events themselves, you may acquire a great degree of cortex-based control over your anxiety. We explored cognitive fusion, which is merely a situation when we forget that our ideas are only thoughts. Consider the case of Maria, a newlywed with a son. At some point in the future, she realized how helpless her infant was and how easy she might do damage to him. At this point, she began to have visions and ideas of the many ways she might harm her kid, whether on purpose or accidentally. She imagined how easy she might drown him if she dropped him by mistake. She was scared to be alone with her kid because she feared she might act on the terrible ideas and visions that had haunted her for so long. She could not tell the difference between what she was thinking and what was happening. It is clear from the fact that she was terrified to spend any time alone with her little kid that she was worried about his safety and would do everything she could to ensure his safety.

Even if the brain generates a wide range of ideas in each of us at any given moment, this does not imply that the thoughts are accurate, that what we are imagining will come to pass, or that we will act on them. We might easily forget that ideas are only neuronal activities in the brain, which have no bearing on reality. The ability to distinguish between ideas and real occurrences is critical to coping with anxiety located in the cortex.

Assessing Your Cognitive Fusion Predispositions

If you have a predisposition to trust your ideas and emotions, you may be hindering your capacity to rewire your brain to resist worry. You must be willing to take advantage of the cortex's high adaptability.

Contemplative Thoughts Adaptation

Ideas or remarks which are likely to have a favorable impact on your emotional state are known as coping thoughts. Examining the impact ideas have on your experience is one method to evaluate their usefulness. You can understand the importance of coping ideas in this light, as they raise the likelihood of calm responses and the capacity to deal with challenging circumstances.

Naturally, you will have to look for ideas that trigger anxiety and replace them with healthy coping mechanisms, but the work will be worth it. Posting coping ideas online might serve as a helpful self-reminder for some individuals. You may reprogram your brain to create coping ideas on its own by considering coping thoughts at every potential moment. Keeping in mind that you are rewiring your brain is important!

Replacing Thoughts

It is common for individuals trying to alter their thinking patterns to lament their inability to do so. When it comes to the human mind, this is a typical issue. Studies have demonstrated that suppressing or erasing a thought is not efficient in achieving the desired outcome. The picture of pink elephants, for example, will naturally spring into your mind if you are asked not to think about them even though you haven't been thinking about them all day. When you attempt to forget about pink elephants, you often think about them, which is paradoxical. This is a pattern that many people with a propensity to fixation are acquainted with. The circuitry that stores an idea is activated and strengthened when you repeatedly tell yourself not to think about it.

You may be able to stop yourself from thinking by reminding yourself. Thought pausing is the name given to this method. The second step, on the other hand, is critical. It is more probable that you will forget the original notion if you focus on anything else instead of it. Working in your garden, imagine you are always looking for snakes. Start thinking about anything else, like a song playing on the radio or the names of flowers you'd want to grow in your garden — basically, anything interesting and, preferably, pleasurable. It is more probable that you won't think about the anxiety-inducing notion again if you focus your attention on anything else.

"Don't erase — replace!" is the greatest strategy for anxiety-inducing thoughts. Try thinking, "I can handle this." instead, "I can't manage this." Now try thinking, I'm certain I can handle this. You will develop a more adaptable mindset and activate circuitry to avoid being anxious with practice. Your new thinking will soon become second nature when you put in the time and effort.

Directions for your Anxiety Channel

Anxiety-inducing behaviors are common in certain individuals. They have a knack for conjuring up horrible situations and are skilled at visualizing the worst-case scenario. It is very uncommon for creative and imaginative folks to suffer from anxiety because of this. The amygdala responds to the way individuals think about their lives and envisage situations, a common occurrence. An example of this is someone who focuses on the worst-case scenario or uses their right brain images in a manner that scares them.

Imagine your brain as a cable TV provider if this is a problem. You cannot leave the Anxiety Channel, even though there are hundreds of channels. In any case, you seem to have chosen it. Anxiety-inducing ideas and pictures may enter your mind without your awareness. Perhaps you are aware of this concentration but disagree with the concepts, much as you would dispute with broadcast political analysts.

Playing games is a great way to keep yourself entertained. It is no wonder that so many nervous individuals find it difficult to let their guard down and have some fun since their misery consumes them. It is critical to cultivating a spirit of fun and silliness. And you do not have to wait till you are no longer tense to have fun. Laughter is the best medicine. Some of the finest diversions are playing games, laughing, and participating in foolishness. It is impossible to go through life's trials without a sense of humor.

If you feel anxious, changing the channel may help alleviate it right away. Increasing the activity in new circuits and decreasing the activity in circuits focused on anxiety-producing themes or pictures is an additional benefit of consciously shifting your attention away from anxiety-igniting ideas. Your brain's wiring strengthens as you utilize it more, whereas the circuitry you do not use deteriorates and becomes less likely to be triggered. Your cortex is rewired for a little period and the rest of your life.

Using Planning to Replace Worry

One of the most enticing aspects of the brain's workings is the ability to worry. For persons prone to anxiety, thinking about an issue, concern, or duty and spending time preparing for the worst is frequently a beneficial strategy. Is it truly beneficial if your amygdala is continually activated by concentrating on your worries?

The earlier chapter helped us understand how it is easy to be sucked into a spiral of anxiety, envisioning bad things and mulling overall answers. A lot of time is wasted worrying about things that may or may not ever happen rather than making plans for what may or may not happen. People's emotional response to a traumatic experience is prolonged when they dwell on the memory of the event for longer than they would have otherwise done.

To avoid becoming bogged down in anxiety or rumination, have a plan! If you know that a problem may develop, brainstorm remedies before moving on to anything else. You can put your strategy into action if the need arises. You do not have to worry about it at this point.

Medicinal Considerations

You may find it useful to take some drugs in your efforts to alter your thinking patterns. Taking benzodiazepines reduces your brain's ability to develop new circuitry, so studies show that those who do not take the drugs gain the most from treatment.

At this stage, a comparison with gardening could be helpful. Fertilizing a garden by taking Selective serotonin reuptake inhibitor SSRIs and Serotonin-norepinephrine reuptake inhibitor SNRIs is like applying fertilizer. There will be an increase in the number of roots, branches, and buds to be seen. It is important to remember that weeds may react to fertilizer rapidly, if not sooner. Similarly, to get the maximum benefit from SSRI or SNRI medication, it is critical to be extremely selective about reinforcing which neural pathways. When you take these drugs, you need to think about what you are teaching your cortex. They are most effective when combined with psychotherapy that focuses on altering negative beliefs.

Taking Care of the Right Psychic Hemisphere

Rewiring your cortex to utilize more of the left hemisphere if the right hemisphere is causing you to worry may assist. Positive emotions and avoidance are the purviews of the right hemisphere, while the left hemisphere is more concerned with how to get to the heart of a person's interests. Play games, watch comedies, and read thought-provoking articles to engage your left hemisphere. Exercise is another great option. These activities can potentially lessen the predominance of reactivity based on the right hemisphere. Mindfulness, which we will examine momentarily, has been found to boost activity in the left hemisphere when practiced.

Another strategy is actively involving the right hemisphere in anything compatible with a low mood state, such as reading or writing. Good examples are listening to upbeat music. A not musically inclined person tends to process music more on the right side of the brain than the left. (Expanding one's left hemispheric abilities via the practice of musical performance) Listening to music that you like activates the right hemisphere of your brain, which is responsible for favorable emotional responses. In addition to speaking, you may want to try singing, which is more likely to stimulate the right hemisphere than speaking. One of the best right hemispheric strategies for combating anxiety is to use music to lift your spirits, boost your energy, and replace any negative thoughts you may be having.

The right hemisphere may be engaged in an activity incompatible with anxiety by using positive imagery. Your right hemisphere is engaged when you use your imagination to transport yourself to a nice place and visualize it in sensory detail. Use your right hemisphere's sensory capabilities by visualizing a happy scenario. It is a wonderful and cheap break from stress.

Putting Mindfulness to Work

Anxiety has the power to take over your brain, your mindful consciousness, and your whole life if you allow it to. How about using the cortex to look at your fear and observe it from a distance rather than being imprisoned by its influence? Would it not be great if you could put yourself outside of the worry by using your cortex? Mindfulness is a brain-based strategy that does this.

Mindfulness is a discipline that has been around for thousands of years and has been practiced in many different cultures. There are so many different ways it may be explained and defined. Anxiety may be conquered by the practice of mindful awareness, according to psychologist Jeffrey Brantley in his book Calming Your Anxious Mind (2007), which discusses the practice. When faced with worry, our instinctive reaction is to attempt to avoid it, suppress it, or even get entangled. When you are open to and accepting of whatever you are experiencing, mindfulness provides you with an alternative route that has its roots in Eastern meditation techniques. It is not always a bad idea to pay attention to "negative thoughts," as psychologist Steven Hayes (2004) puts it. One way to think about it is to teach your cortex to notice your anxiety reactions with love and patience, similar to how a loving parent could witness a kid's temper tantrum and stay kind and nonreactive until the youngster settles down.

Essentially, mindfulness is a technique of embracing the present moment and seeing it in a new manner: with a focus on letting, accepting, and being completely aware of whatever you are feeling at any given time. Although it may seem to be an easy task, it requires a lot of experience. However, you may include this exercise in your daily routine. When you eat breakfast, listen to the birds in your yard, stroll, or focus on your breathing, you may all serve as chances to practice mindfulness. As soon as you pay attention to them, you will notice the difference. Observing how frequently you are entangled in ideas can let you see how much of life you are missing out on. An example of this is a female.

When you have mastered carefully watching daily events, you may begin to concentrate on your worry. While practicing mindfulness, you learn to separate yourself from your worry and its accompanying bodily symptoms in favor of seeing the world objectively, without judgment, as a tranquil observer.

Putting All the Pieces Together for Anxiety-Free Living

Hopefully, the information you have gained from this book will aid you in achieving a better quality of life in the future. Your anxiety is not entirely under your control, but understanding how the amygdala creates it and how the cortical route contributes to it helps. You have no control over how your brain is wired to make you anxious. You can, however, learn to manage your worry. Many studies have shown the brain's neuroplasticity, which means it can rewire your brain to feel less worried.

You do not have to let worry rule your life just because you cannot control certain elements of it. Anxiety will never go away for anybody, but there are ways to lessen its grip on our lives by focusing on both the amygdala and the cortex of our brains.

Increasing Your Willpower

There is a lot of information presented here, but it can be broken down into small chunks. As you progress, you will be encouraged by the progress you are seeing. You will have more self-confidence in dealing with your anxiety once you have used the relaxation techniques. You will be encouraged when you see positive changes in your thinking due to these methods. You will be able to face your anxieties more and more when you begin to see how exposure lessens your anxiety.

Remember that the ultimate aim is to rewire your brain, so pay attention to how your brain responds to each stage. When you apply a strategy, you send a message to your brain, and your brain will eventually adjust. Do not be scared off by having to practice all the time. After all, this is a prerequisite for success in almost every field, from mathematics to sports. Step by step, you are taking control of your life. Inevitably, you will encounter difficulties. To maintain your resolve, consider using the following suggestions.

Despite Your Fear, Take Action!

It is easier said than done to take action in the face of fear. When you think about it, that's exactly what you need to do to change your perception of anxiety and change your brain. Courage is doing action despite your fear, so remember that.

The information in this book has given you a better understanding of anxiety. Complex neural mechanisms underlie this diverse sensation. If you have learned anything about anxiety, you will face folks who have no idea what you have learned about it. Do not let other people's opinions stop you from pursuing your dreams. Before lunch, you may experience more terror than most people do in a year. While others may not realize this, getting to the plate for you entails jogging six or seven bases instead of simply four. Because of this, giving yourself credit for what you are doing may be quite beneficial. Your companions may have no idea that going out with them is more of a labor of love than a fun night out. Take satisfaction in the accomplishments you have made despite your anxieties.

Take It One Day at a Time

Life should be taken one day at a time, and we urge you to do so. When this is used in daily life, it involves letting go of concerns about what could or might not happen in the future. Focusing on the here and now allows you to save your mental energy for the job at hand. There is no use in looking back at unpleasant events from your past and worrying about what could happen in the future when you might be doing something more productive. Staying on the Anxiety Channel may cause you to miss out on some of life's most memorable moments.

Focusing on one minute at a time may be useful while under pressure. In some cases, the only thing we can handle is to get through a single moment. Focusing on one problem at a time is perfectly reasonable. If you are lucky, you are only given one second at a time to live your life. When faced with worry, the only thing that matters is getting through the minute. Simply getting through a few minutes is a significant accomplishment in other cases. One minute at a time is sometimes a good way to tackle life.

6.4 Try Being More Optimistic

Many events in your life are unique to you. You will be happy if you can learn to concentrate your thoughts on pleasant events and relish them. Listen to the moments of happiness and beauty that come your way, and hang on to them. Playfulness is a virtue to cultivate. Love the ones you have. When it comes down to it, love is more powerful than fear.

When things go wrong, it is an indication that you are pushing yourself to the limit. Ships are safe in harbors, but that is not where they are designed to remain. Likely, you are not aiming high enough if you never experience setbacks. There is no need to concentrate on setbacks, shapes or forms. If you are willing to look, you can discover joy and beauty in the world around you. Feel the joy you receive from these rare occasions as you enjoy them consciously and intentionally. Your brain is greatly influenced by how you concentrate your thoughts. Make a point of focusing on the good things in your life. As a consequence, you will be happy.

Keep Hold of Your Anxiety

If you have anxiety, you can learn to manage it, regardless of how you got your anxiety issues in the first place: genetics or life events. Anxiety circuits can be rewired using the techniques in this book, even if they are already engaged in your brain. Keep your mind on the good and avoid letting anxiousness take over. With the information you have received from this book, you will be able to better control your anxiety and rewire your brain so that it no longer triggers anxiety attacks.

Conclusion

Many people feel that their stress is exacerbated by thoughts about the current stress and prior events or concerns and situations that may happen in the future.

If you have ever been stressed, you may have observed that the same ideas repeat themselves in your mind, producing an endless cycle and increasing your anxiety. This thinking process would do nothing to assist in resolving the difficulties at hand, but it can also get in the way of healthy habits that can help you achieve inner calm, such as getting enough sleep.

It seems like tackling the issue of anxious thoughts is not that difficult after all and it can be done simply by following the suggestions of experts in the field. The book **Mastering your Anxious Brain** is a complete package for finding a solution to such issues and many others. It is important to change how to spend your days and nights by giving maximum time to positive thinking and actions that are helpful for yourself and the people around you.

The thumb rule is to try being more optimistic and give as little space as possible to negative thoughts. It can be done by showing empathy and compassion towards others and always being ready to help people. Helping others will bring a feeling of relaxation and you will feel motivated to do much better in your life.

www.ingramcontent.com/pod-product-compliance
Lightning Source LLC
Chambersburg PA
CBHW071013120626
46546CB00003B/1064